First World War
and Army of Occupation
War Diary
France, Belgium and Germany

56 DIVISION
Divisional Troops
281 Brigade Royal Field Artillery
1 September 1915 - 25 May 1919

WO95/2940/3

The Naval & Military Press Ltd
www.nmarchive.com
Published in association with The National Archives

Published by

The Naval & Military Press Ltd

Unit 10 Ridgewood Industrial Park,

Uckfield, East Sussex,

TN22 5QE England

Tel: +44 (0) 1825 749494

www.naval-military-press.com

www.nmarchive.com

This diary has been reprinted in facsimile from the original. Any imperfections are inevitably reproduced and the quality may fall short of modern type and cartographic standards.

© **Crown Copyright**
Images reproduced by permission of The National Archives, London, England, 2015.

Contents

Document type	Place/Title	Date From	Date To
Heading	WO95/2940/3		
Heading	56 Division Troops 281 Brigade R.F.A. (Formerly 1/2 London Bde) 1915 Aug-1919 May (Missing 1917-Jly To Sep)		
Heading	56 Div Troops 1/2nd London Bde RFA 1915 Sep-1915 Dec		
Miscellaneous	War Statement No.12	31/08/1915	31/08/1915
Miscellaneous	War Statement No.13	30/09/1915	30/09/1915
War Diary	Saxmundham	01/09/1915	14/09/1915
War Diary	Sutton Common	15/09/1915	15/09/1915
War Diary	Saxmundham	17/09/1915	23/09/1915
War Diary	Bordon	24/09/1915	30/09/1915
Heading	36th Division 1/2nd London Bde. R.F.A. Vol I Oct 15		
Heading	War Diary Of 1/2 London Brigade R.F.A. From 1st Oct To 31st Oct 1915		
War Diary	Bordon	02/10/1915	02/10/1915
War Diary	Southamton	03/10/1915	03/10/1915
War Diary	Harve	04/10/1915	04/10/1915
War Diary	Longueau	05/10/1915	05/10/1915
War Diary	Villers Bocage	05/10/1915	09/10/1915
War Diary	Thievres	10/10/1915	10/10/1915
War Diary	Sailly Au Bois	10/10/1915	18/10/1915
War Diary	Sailly	19/10/1915	19/10/1915
War Diary	Thievres	20/10/1915	20/10/1915
War Diary	Villers Bocage	21/10/1915	21/10/1915
War Diary	Bonnville	22/10/1915	22/10/1915
War Diary	Berneuil	23/10/1915	30/10/1915
Heading	War Diary Of 1/2 London Brigade R.F.A. From 1st Nov 1915 To 30th Nov 1915		
Heading	56 Div 1/2 London Bde R.F.A. Nov Vol II		
War Diary	Berneuil	01/11/1915	28/11/1915
War Diary	Franqueville	29/11/1915	10/12/1915
War Diary	Pontremy	11/12/1915	11/12/1915
War Diary	Boeseghem	12/12/1915	21/12/1915
War Diary	Laventie	22/12/1915	30/12/1915
Heading	1-2nd London Brigade RFA Jan-Feb 1916		
War Diary	Laventie	31/12/1915	31/12/1915
War Diary	Lieres	01/01/1916	04/01/1916
War Diary	Verquin	05/01/1916	05/01/1916
War Diary	Philosophe	06/01/1916	06/01/1916
War Diary	Mazingarbe Brewery	06/01/1916	10/01/1916
War Diary	Mazingarbe	11/01/1916	31/01/1916
Heading	1/2nd Lon. Bde. R.F.A. War Diary For Month Of Feby 1916 Vol III		
War Diary	Mazingarbe	01/02/1916	17/02/1916
War Diary	Marles	18/02/1916	21/02/1916
War Diary	Lillers	24/02/1916	24/02/1916
War Diary	Allery	25/02/1916	26/02/1916
War Diary	L'Etoile	27/02/1916	27/02/1916
Miscellaneous	Col Poole Commanding Counter Battery Group	15/02/1916	15/02/1916

Miscellaneous	My Dear Macdowell	18/02/1916	18/02/1916
Miscellaneous	1st London Divisional Artillery	22/02/1916	22/02/1916
Miscellaneous	London Divisional Arty	29/02/1916	29/02/1916
Heading	1/2nd London Bde R.F.A. War Diary For March 1916 Vol IV		
War Diary	L'Etoile	28/02/1916	12/03/1916
War Diary	Candas	15/03/1916	15/03/1916
War Diary	Berlencourt	16/03/1916	30/03/1916
Heading	1/2nd Lon. Bde. RFA War Diary Month Of April 1916 Vol V		
War Diary	Berlencourt	31/03/1916	30/04/1916
Heading	81st Brigade R.F.A. Late 1/2 London Bde RFA War Diary From 1st May To 30th May 1916		
War Diary	Berlencourt	01/05/1916	03/05/1916
War Diary	Sailly & Pas	06/05/1916	09/05/1916
War Diary	Sailly	12/05/1916	25/05/1916
War Diary	Hebuterne	26/05/1916	27/05/1916
War Diary	Sailly	28/05/1916	29/05/1916
Operation(al) Order(s)	Operation Order No. 2 Relief Of 48th Divisional Artillery by 56th Divisional Artillery	06/05/1916	06/05/1916
Miscellaneous	Plan For R.A.	25/05/1916	25/05/1916
Miscellaneous	With Reference To Operations For Advancement Of Trench Lines On 56th Divisional Front	25/05/1916	25/05/1916
Miscellaneous	The Officer Commanding Heavy Artillery Group	23/05/1916	23/05/1916
Operation(al) Order(s)	Operation Order No. I.D.42 by Lt. Col. C.C. Macdowell, Commanding 56th. Div. Artillery Group.		
Miscellaneous	Special Operations By The 56th Division To Be held On a date To Be notified later	24/05/1916	24/05/1916
Operation(al) Order(s)	Operation Order No. I.D. 48 by Lt. Col. C.C. Macdowell, Commanding 56th. Div. Art. Group.	26/05/1916	26/05/1916
Operation(al) Order(s)	Operation Order No I.D 49 by Lt. Col. C.C. Macdowell, Commdg 56th. Div. Arty. Group.	27/05/1916	27/05/1916
Operation(al) Order(s)	Operation Order No I.D 46 by Lt. Col. C.C. Macdowell, Commdg 56th. Div. Arty. Group.	25/05/1916	25/05/1916
Miscellaneous	G.O.C 56th Division	28/05/1916	28/05/1916
Miscellaneous	167th Infantry Bde.	28/05/1916	28/05/1916
Heading	281st Brigade RFA War Diary Month Of June 1916 Vol 7		
War Diary	Sailly	01/06/1916	30/06/1916
Operation(al) Order(s)	Operation Order No. I.D. 80 by Lt. Col. C.C. Macdowell, Commanding Southern Artillery Group.		
Miscellaneous	Notes		
Miscellaneous	U Day		
Miscellaneous	V Day		
Miscellaneous	W Day		
Miscellaneous	X Day		
Miscellaneous	Y Day		
Miscellaneous	Bombardment Of Bucquoy		
Operation(al) Order(s)	Operation Order No. 4 by Brigadier General R.J.G. Elkington C.M.G. Commanding 56th Divisional Artillery.	20/06/1916	20/06/1916
Miscellaneous	Amendments	24/06/1916	24/06/1916
Miscellaneous	O.P's And Suspected O.P's	24/06/1916	24/06/1916
Miscellaneous	Operation Orders by Lt Col C.C. MacDowell Commanding the Macart Group	28/06/1916	28/06/1916

Type	Description	Date From	Date To
Operation(al) Order(s)	Operation Order (No. 6) by Brigadier General Elkington. C.M.G. Commanding 56th Divisional Artillery.	28/06/1916	28/06/1916
Miscellaneous	Special 56th Divisional Order	28/06/1916	28/06/1916
Miscellaneous	Operation Ordered For "Z" Day (to-morrow) are cancelled and the following substituted-:	28/06/1916	28/06/1916
Miscellaneous	Operation Orders by Lt Col C.C. MacDowell Commanding the Macart Group		
Miscellaneous	Z Day Before Zero Time		
Heading	281st Brigade RFA War Diary For Month Of July 1916		
War Diary	Hebuterne	01/07/1916	01/07/1916
War Diary	Sailly	04/07/1916	18/07/1916
War Diary	Hebuterne	18/07/1916	18/07/1916
War Diary	Sailly	19/07/1916	19/07/1916
War Diary	Pas	20/07/1916	29/07/1916
Miscellaneous	Appendix A		
Miscellaneous	Barrages A Battery		
Miscellaneous	Barrages B Battery		
Miscellaneous	Barrages C Battery		
Miscellaneous	Barrages D How. Battery		
Miscellaneous	Barrages 109th Battery		
Miscellaneous	Appendix B Bombardment.		
Miscellaneous	Appendix C		
Miscellaneous	56th Division	03/07/1916	03/07/1916
Miscellaneous	General Officer Commanding Third Army	17/07/1916	17/07/1916
Miscellaneous	Appendix C 56th. Division. S.G. 121/91.	15/07/1916	15/07/1916
Heading	56th Divisional Brigade 281st Brigade Royal Field Artillery August 1916		
War Diary	Sailly	06/08/1916	31/08/1916
Miscellaneous	56th Division	19/08/1916	19/08/1916
Miscellaneous	Operation Orders by Lt Col C.C. MacDowell Commanding Southern Group 56th Div Artillery	28/08/1916	28/08/1916
Miscellaneous	Further To I.D No. 167	30/08/1916	30/08/1916
Operation(al) Order(s)	Operation Orders No. 167 by Lt Col C.C. MacDowell Commanding 281st Brigade R.F.A.	30/08/1916	30/08/1916
Heading	56th Divisional Artillery 281st (Late 2nd London) Brigade R.F.A. September 1916		
War Diary	Pas	01/09/1916	01/09/1916
War Diary	Outre Bois	02/09/1916	02/09/1916
War Diary	Rainneville	04/09/1916	04/09/1916
War Diary	Daours	05/09/1916	05/09/1916
War Diary	Bray	06/09/1916	11/09/1916
War Diary	Hardecourt	12/09/1916	30/09/1916
Miscellaneous	Right Group Left Group	26/09/1916	26/09/1916
Miscellaneous		26/09/1916	26/09/1916
Miscellaneous	All Units		
Miscellaneous	56th Division G.932	18/09/1916	18/09/1916
War Diary	Hardecourt	01/11/1916	02/11/1916
War Diary	Mametz	03/11/1916	03/11/1916
War Diary	Daours	04/11/1916	04/11/1916
War Diary	Rebreuviette	05/11/1916	06/11/1916
War Diary	Berthonval Farm	07/11/1916	30/11/1916
Miscellaneous	56th Divisional Artillery	25/10/1916	25/10/1916
Miscellaneous	Appendix A	10/11/1916	10/11/1916
Heading	281st Bde. R.F.A. War Diary For December 1916		
War Diary	Berthonval St Eloi	01/12/1916	01/12/1916

War Diary	ACQ	02/12/1916	02/12/1916
War Diary	Raimbert	03/12/1916	03/12/1916
War Diary	Haverskerque	04/12/1916	08/12/1916
War Diary	Lavantie	08/12/1916	28/12/1916
Heading	War Diary Of 281st Brigade R.F.A. From 1/1/17 To 31/1/17		
War Diary	Laventie	01/01/1917	31/01/1917
Heading	War Diary Of 281st Brigade R.F.A. (Late 1/2nd London Brigade R.F.A.) For The Period 1st-28th February 1917 Vol 15		
War Diary	Laventie	02/02/1917	27/02/1917
Heading	War Diary Of 281st Brigade R.F.A. T.F. (Late 1/2nd City Of London Brigade R.F.A. T.F.) For The Period 1st To 31st March 1917 Vol 16		
War Diary	Laventie	03/03/1917	05/03/1917
War Diary	Calonne	06/03/1917	07/03/1917
War Diary	Liettres	08/03/1917	08/03/1917
War Diary	Heuchin	09/03/1917	09/03/1917
War Diary	Conchy	10/03/1917	13/03/1917
War Diary	Arras	14/03/1917	19/03/1917
War Diary	Beaurains	20/03/1917	31/03/1917
Heading	War Diary Of 281st Brigade R.F.A. T.F Late 1st/2nd London Brigade R.F.A. T.F. For The Period April 1st To 30th 1917 Vol 17		
War Diary	Beaurains	01/04/1917	10/04/1917
War Diary	Beaurains Mercatel Road M.23.a	11/04/1917	11/04/1917
War Diary	Neuville Vitasse	12/04/1917	12/04/1917
War Diary	S' Martin Sur Cojeul	13/04/1917	30/04/1917
Heading	War Diary Of 281st Brigade R.F.A. Late 1/2nd London Brigade R.F.A.T.F For The Period May 1st-May 31st 1917		
War Diary	St Martin-Sur-Cojeul (Hindenburg Line)	01/05/1917	31/05/1917
Miscellaneous	18th Div. Artillery	28/05/1917	28/05/1917
Heading	War Diary For Month Of June 1917 Vol 19 281st Bde R.F.A.		
War Diary	St Martin Sur Cojeul Hindenburg Line	01/06/1917	04/06/1917
War Diary	Henin Sur Cojeul	05/06/1917	09/06/1917
War Diary	Hendecourt	10/06/1917	13/06/1917
War Diary	Near St Leger	14/06/1917	18/06/1917
War Diary	Henin Sur Cojeul Hindenburg Line	19/06/1917	19/06/1917
War Diary	Henin Sur Cojeul and Heninel	20/06/1917	24/06/1917
War Diary	Henin Sur Cojeul	25/06/1917	27/06/1917
War Diary	Hendecourt	28/06/1917	30/06/1917
Heading	War Diary Of 281st Brigade R.F.A. Late 1/2nd London Brigade R.F.A.T.F. For The Period October 1st To 31st 1917		
War Diary	Morchies	01/10/1917	29/10/1917
Heading	War Diary Of 281st Brigade R.F.A. (Late 1/2nd London Brigade R.F.A.T.F) For The Period From 1st November 1917 To 30th November 1917		
War Diary	Morchies	02/11/1917	30/11/1917
Heading	War Diary Of 281st Brigade R.F.A. (Late 1/2nd London Bde RFA) For The Period 1st-31st December 1917 Vol 25		
War Diary	Morchies	01/12/1917	06/12/1917
War Diary	Vaulx	07/12/1917	14/12/1917

War Diary	Noreuil	14/12/1917	15/12/1917
War Diary	Behagnies	15/12/1917	15/12/1917
War Diary	Montenescourt	16/12/1917	16/12/1917
War Diary	Berles	17/12/1917	19/12/1917
War Diary	Bailleul	19/12/1917	31/12/1917
Miscellaneous	H.Q 56 Div. Arty	31/01/1918	31/01/1918
Heading	War Diary 281st Bde RFA January 1918 Vol 26		
War Diary	Vimy Ridge Bailleul	01/01/1918	06/01/1918
War Diary	Bailluel	09/01/1918	19/01/1918
War Diary	Aubigny	21/01/1918	22/01/1918
Heading	War Diary Month February 1918 Vol 27		
War Diary	Aubigny	01/02/1918	15/02/1918
War Diary	Vimy Ridge Bailleul	16/02/1918	28/02/1918
Heading	Headquarters 281st Brigade, R.F.A. March 1918		
Heading	War Diary Of 281st Brigade R.F.A. Late 1/2nd London Brigade R.F.A. For The Period March 1st To March 31st 1918 Vol 28		
War Diary	Bailleul	01/03/1918	01/03/1918
War Diary	E. Of Arras	02/03/1918	12/03/1918
War Diary	Bailleul	13/03/1918	31/03/1918
Heading	56th Divisional Artillery (Late 1/2nd London Bde R.F.A.) 281st Brigade R.F.A. April 1918		
War Diary	Vimy Ridge Bailleul	01/04/1918	07/04/1918
War Diary	Achicourt Near Arras	08/04/1918	14/04/1918
War Diary	Ronville Caves Arras	15/04/1918	29/04/1918
War Diary	Boulevaid Carnot Arras	30/04/1918	30/04/1918
Miscellaneous	Appendix A	28/03/1918	28/03/1918
Heading	281 Bde RFA War Diary Month Of May 1918 Vol 30		
War Diary	Arras Ronville Caves	01/05/1918	11/05/1918
War Diary	Arras Boulevard Carnot	12/05/1918	30/05/1918
Miscellaneous	Appendix A O.C. Right Group. R.A.	20/05/1918	20/05/1918
Heading	War Diary Of The 281st Brigade R.F.A. (Late 1/2nd London Brigade RFA T.F.) For The Period 1st To 30th June 1918 Vol 31		
War Diary	Boulevard Carnot Arras	01/06/1918	01/06/1918
War Diary	Wgn Lines Simoncourt	01/06/1918	03/06/1918
War Diary	Arras	04/06/1918	15/06/1918
War Diary	Wagon Lines Simoncourt	15/06/1918	23/06/1918
War Diary	Arras	24/06/1918	29/06/1918
Heading	War Diary Of The 281st Brigade R.F.A. Late 1/2nd London Bde. For The Period From 1st July 1918 To 31st July 1918 Vol 32		
War Diary	Boulevard Carnot	01/07/1918	01/07/1918
War Diary	Arras	02/07/1918	21/07/1918
War Diary	Simoncourt	22/07/1918	22/07/1918
War Diary	ACQ	23/07/1918	31/07/1918
Heading	War Diary Of 281st Brigade R.F.A. Late 1/2nd London Brigade R.F.A.T.F For The Period August 1st To 31st 1918 Vol 33		
Miscellaneous	Cover For Documents. Nature Of Enclosures.		
War Diary	Simoncourt	01/08/1918	01/08/1918
War Diary	Arras	02/08/1918	15/08/1918
War Diary	Simoncourt	16/08/1918	22/08/1918
War Diary	Blairville	23/08/1918	23/08/1918
War Diary	Boiseux Au Mond	24/08/1918	24/08/1918
War Diary	Boyelles	25/08/1918	29/08/1918

War Diary	St Leger	29/08/1918	31/08/1918
Heading	War Diary Of 281st Brigade R.F.A. Late 1/2nd London Brigade R.F.A.T.F. For The Period 1st To 30th September 1918		
War Diary	St Leger	01/09/1918	02/09/1918
War Diary	Queant	03/09/1918	05/09/1918
War Diary	St Leger	06/09/1918	07/09/1918
War Diary	St Martin Sur Cojeul	08/09/1918	08/09/1918
War Diary	Eterpigny	09/09/1918	18/09/1918
War Diary	Dury	19/09/1918	30/09/1918
Heading	War Diary 281st Brigade R.F.A. (Late 2nd London Bde R.F.A.T.F) Vol 35		
War Diary	Dury	01/10/1918	03/10/1918
War Diary	Oisy Le Verger	04/10/1918	17/10/1918
War Diary	Ecourt St Quentin	18/10/1918	18/10/1918
War Diary	Aubigny-Au-Bac	19/10/1918	19/10/1918
War Diary	Marcq	20/10/1918	20/10/1918
War Diary	Eswars	21/10/1918	28/10/1918
War Diary	Thiant	29/10/1918	31/10/1918
Heading	War Diary 281 Brigade R.F.A. Month Of November 1918 Vol 36		
War Diary	Miang	01/11/1918	01/11/1918
War Diary	Famars	02/11/1918	02/11/1918
War Diary	Saultain	03/11/1918	04/11/1918
War Diary	Sebourg	05/11/1918	06/11/1918
War Diary	Angreau	07/11/1918	07/11/1918
War Diary	Honnezies Fayt Le Franc	08/11/1918	08/11/1918
War Diary	Blaregnies	09/11/1918	10/11/1918
War Diary	Convent Query Le Petit	11/11/1918	26/11/1918
War Diary	Vieuxreng	27/11/1918	30/11/1918
Heading	281st Brigade R.F.A. War Diary Month Of December 1918 Vol 37		
War Diary	Chateau Rouvroy	16/12/1918	25/12/1918
War Diary	Vieux Rang	08/12/1918	09/12/1918
War Diary	Chateau Rouvroy	10/12/1918	12/12/1918
War Diary	Chateau Rouvroy Belgium	01/01/1919	28/02/1919
War Diary	Rouveroy	11/03/1919	15/03/1919
War Diary	Mesvin	17/03/1919	29/03/1919
War Diary	Mesvin near Mons	06/04/1919	30/04/1919
War Diary	Quaregnon Belgium	25/05/1919	25/05/1919
Miscellaneous	Duplicate Confidential		

WO 95/2940/3

BEF

56 DIVISION TROOPS

281 BRIGADE R.F.A
(FORMERLY 1/2 LONDON BDE)

1915 AUG — 1919 MAY

(MISSING 1917, JLY TO SEP)

Box 2940

56 DIV TRAINS

FORMED 36 + 38 DIVS
1/2nd London Bde RFA
~~Oct~~ Dec 1915
1915 SEP - 1915 DEC

WAR STATEMENT No.12.   31st. August 1915.

1/2nd. LONDON BRIGADE R.F.A. (Less 1/6th. COUNTY OF LONDON BATTERY).

AND ("C" SUB-SECTION AMMUNITION COLUMN ATTACHED).

MOBOLIZATION CENTRE.	WOOLWICH.	
TEMPORARY WAR STATION.	WHITMOOR COMMON SURREY.	From 27th. August to 8th. September 1914.
STATIONS SINCE OCCUPIED.	MARESFIELD PARK SUSSEX.	From 14th. September to 17th. November 1914.
	HORHSEA, EAST YORKSHIRE.	Headquarters from 19/11/14 to 20/4/15. Left Section of 1/5th. County of London Battery and proportion of Ammunition Column from 19/11/14 to 15/1/15. 1/4th. County of London Battery from 16/1/15 to 20/4/15.
	WITHERNSEA. EAST YORKSHIRE.	Right Section of 1/5th. County of London Battery from 19/11/14 to 20/4/15 and proportion of Ammunition Column 19/11/14 to 15/1/15. Left Section of 1/5th. Battery from 16/1/15 to 20/4/15.
	FILEY.	Left Section 1/4th. County of London Battery and proportion of Ammunition Column from 19/11/14 to 15/1/1915.
	BRIDLINGTON.	Right Section of 1/4th. County of London Battery and proportion of Ammunition Column from 19/11/14 to 23/11/14.
	BARMSTON.	-ditto- from 24/11/14 to 15/1/15.
	SPROATLEY.	Ammunition Column from 16/1/15 to 20/4/15.
	BURGESS HILL.	Headquarters, 1/4th. Battery and 1/5th. Battery, and Ammunition Column from 24/4/15 to 16/5/15.
	HORSHAM ST FAITHS.	Headquarters, 1/4th. Bty. and 1/5th. Battery from 17/5/15 to 16/8/15.
	RACKHEATH PARK.	Ammunition Column from 17/5/15 to 2/8/15.
	BROME.	Ammunition Column from 3/8/15 to 16/8/15.
	SAXMUNDHAM.	Hd.Qtrs., 1/4th., 1/5th., Batteries & Am. Column from 16/8/15 to...........

(b) CONCENTRATION AT WAR STATIONS. The Brigade concentrated at SAXMUNDHAM on the 17th. The moves took place by road and were carried out much better than any previous ones. Shoeing proved to be good as only one had to be attended to on the road. It would perhaps be an advantage to start earlier than 8.am. for a 20 mile march, especially as owing to shortage of horses, the Batteries could not go out of a walk at all.

(d) TRAINING. Much time has been occupied in training those attached from the 2/2nd. London R.F.A., and also Transport Drivers from the 175th. Infantry Bde. There is not any suitable ground for manoeuvring here, but we are very fortunate in having the Park here for training those attached.

(e) DISCIPLINE. Good. No serious crime.

(f) ADMINISTRATION.
MEDICAL SERVICES. (1) Well carried out by the M.O. i/c of the Brigade as far as he can go. One man who went to Hospital in January was discharged from Hospital on 5th. inst. as medically unfit, but his Discharge has not yet been carried out: meanwhile, he is drawing pay & allowances for dependants. Other men, subject to epileptic fits, mentally deficient, &c &c., for which authority to Discharge cannot be obtained.

VETERINARY SERVICES. (2) Good. Health of Horses very satisfactory.

SUPPLY SERVICES. (3) Satisfactory.

TRANSPORT SERVICES. (4) The Brigade has to do its own, which, including the carting of water, is heavy.

ORDNANCE SERVICES. (5) Some delay in getting some stores. Great delay in getting repairs done at Ipswich where one of our Fitters has been since June, and the Elevating Gear of only one Gun has been returned up to the present.
New Harness (Canadian) has been received. Not as accurately made or as good as English.
The G.S. Wagons (Canadians and American) have to altered to suit the harness. 5 S.A.A. Carts have been received. Telephone Cart (without equipment or harness) has been received. Neither have instructions been received as to the necessary increase of Horses and Drivers for Brigade Headquarters. Still have Nos 60 and 65 Fuzes, which may lead to confusion.

SUPPLY OF REMOUNTS. (9) Have received 100- a good all round lot, and apparently only a few will give trouble.

Saxmundham.
31/8/15.

H.B. Tucker
Lieutenant Colonel.
Commanding 1/2nd. London Brigade R. F. A.

WAR STATEMENT, No.13.   30th September 1915

1/2nd. LONDON BRIGADE ROYAL FIELD ARTILLERY.

MOBILIZATION CENTRE.   WOOLWICH.

TEMPORARY WAR STATION.   SAXMUNDHAM   Head Quarters 1/4th.,
                                                1/5th. Batteries and
                                                Ammunition Column
                                                from 16/8/1915 to 23/9/1915

                              BORDON   From 24th. Septr.

(b) CONCENTRATION.   The Brigade concentrated at BORDON on the 24th.
                              inst. Headquarters, 1/4th. 1/5th., Batteries
                              and Ammunition Column (less "C" subsection)
                              From SAXMUNDHAM, the 1/6th. Battery and C
                              subsection Ammunition Column from TADWORTH.
                              The first time the Brigade has been
                              concentrated since Mobilization at WOOLWICH
                              in August 1914. The move by rail to BORDON
                              was carried out without any casualties.
                              The trains were late in being ready for loading
                              at SAXMUNDHAM.

(d) TRAINING.   Was carried out at SAXMUNDHAM and the general
                              standard was improved. At the same time
                              3 Officers and 150 Other ranks of the 2/2nd.
                              London Brigade R.F.A., were being trained
                              by this Brigade.

(e) DISCIPLINE   Generally Good.

(f) ADMINISTRATION

(1) MEDICAL SERVICES   Satisfactory. Lieutenant Elliott has
                              replaced Captain Wotherspoon since the Brigade
                              arrived here, the latter being for Home
                              Service meantime.

(2) VETERINARY SERVICES.   Good. Lieutenant Townsend had to go on
                              sick leave and meantime Lieutenant Bradley
                              reported for duty. But now the former has
                              returned and it is sincerely hoped he may be
                              allowed to accompany the Brigade Overseas.
                              He knows the horses well and is most
                              industrious and painstaking.

(5) ORDNANCE SERVICES.   Have obtained every assistance possible.

(9) SUPPLY OF REMOUNTS.   Have had all required to complete establishment
                              from the Artillery, which we partly replace,
                              in the 36th. (Ulster) Division.

(h) PREPARATION FOR
    IMPERIAL SERVICE.   Since being here, have been fully occupied
                              in drawing Stores, Equipment, Clothing &c.,
                              for service overseas. The Brigade now has
                              18 pdr. Guns having handed over the 15 pdrs.
                              to the 2/2nd. London Brigade R.F.A.

                                              H.B. Tasker
                                              Lieutenant Colonel
                              Commanding 1/2nd. London Brigade R.F.A.

BORDON.
30-9-1915.

WAR STATEMENT, No.13.   30th. September 1915

1/2nd. LONDON BRIGADE ROYAL FIELD ARTILLERY.

MOBILIZATION CENTRE.   WOOLWICH.

TEMPORARY WAR STATION.   SAXMUNDHAM   Head Quarters 1/4th.,
                                                1/5th. Batteries and
                                                Ammunition Column
                                                from 16/8/1915 to 23/9/1915

                              BORDON   From 24th. Septr.

(b) CONCENTRATION.   The Brigade concentrated at BORDON on the 24th.
                              inst. Headquarters, 1/4th. 1/5th., Batteries
                              and Ammunition Column (less "C" subsection)
                              from SAXMUNDHAM, the 1/6th. Battery and C
                              subsection Ammunition Column from TADWORTH.
                              The first time the Brigade has been
                              concentrated since Mobilization at WOOLWICH
                              in August 1914. The move by rail to BORDON
                              was carried out without any casualties.
                              The trains were late in being ready for loading
                              at SAXMUNDHAM.

(d) TRAINING.   Was carried out at SAXMUNDHAM and the general
                              standard was improved. At the same time
                              3 Officers and 150 Other ranks of the 2/2nd.
                              London Brigade R.F.A., were being trained
                              by this Brigade.

(e) DISCIPLINE   Generally Good.

(f) ADMINISTRATION

(1) MEDICAL SERVICES   Satisfactory. Lieutenant Elliott has
                              replaced Captain Wotherspoon since the Brigade
                              arrived here, the latter being for Home
                              Service meantime.

(2) VETERINARY SERVICES.   Good. Lieutenant Townsend had to go on
                              sick leave and meantime Lieutenant Bradley
                              reported for duty. But now the former has
                              returned and it is sincerely hoped he may be
                              allowed to accompany the Brigade Overseas.
                              He knows the horses well and is most
                              industrious and painstaking.

(5) ORDNANCE SERVICES.   Have obtained every assistance possible.

(9) SUPPLY OF REMOUNTS.   Have had all required to complete establishment
                              from the Artillery, which we partly replace,
                              in the 56th.(Ulster) Division.

(h) PREPARATION FOR
    IMPERIAL SERVICE.   Since being here, have been fully occupied
                              in drawing Stores, Equipment, Clothing &c.,
                              for service overseas. The Brigade now has
                              18 pdr. Guns having handed over the 15 pdrs.
                              to the 2/2nd. London Brigade R.F.A.

                                              Lieutenant Colonel
                                       Commanding 1/2nd. London Brigade R.F.A.

BORDON.
30-9-1915.

WAR DIARY or INTELLIGENCE SUMMARY

Army Form C. 2118

1/2d Lon. Bde R.F.A.

Place	Date	Hour	Summary of Events and Information	Remarks and references to Appendices
SAXMUND-HAM	3/9/15		Horses Transferred 25 having ones from Th Battries in the Bus. Col. This also had the advantage of giving local lead about the remounts having 85 Remounts hard Turnerard 90. We had still at uddend strength actually been 3 weeks and blowered 405	
	5/9/15		Received very freely this ground seems unsuited week weather. Thereare a deficiency of stable equip + central teaching and horses are Lanterne unfit for use Powerme to go in action 5 allowed	
	4/9/15		Sent 3 Horses to the Hotel for Supr Richardson has in accordance with his letter after meeting an can knew what the Horses had been doing 407 Cannot in such a fearful state from the rain cauto do anything except hoping to get a letter 407	
	6/9/15		Raining and Harshly afternoon amoney 407 Remounts Rec't really influenza swamped the attached from 2/2 Lon. Bde returned to Woolwich 407	
	8/9/15			

WAR DIARY
or
INTELLIGENCE SUMMARY

(Erase heading not required.)

Army Form C. 2118

Instructions regarding War Diaries and Intelligence Summaries are contained in F. S. Regs., Part II. and the Staff Manual respectively. Title Pages will be prepared in manuscript.

Place	Date	Hour	Summary of Events and Information	Remarks, and references to Appendices
	8/9/15		Eve 23 returned to refill re 23 wounded officers, O.R. 2/2 Dlrs. Rch Telegraphed awaiting Reserves from Batteries. No reply of Record. A.D.V.S. completed Sick Horses MR?	
	10/9/15		G.O. Notification No. M.R. N7Q sent wait back after measures found 6 h.p. sine Lent 7 moved No 2 Sick horse. The Board of Recreant inspected the horses at wenn the expense of themselves satisfied the believe in 2 of food for horses in backward horses. Folkestone, Dover, Sheffield.	
	11/9/15			
	12/9/15			Broomwell, routed to Broomwell.
	13/9/15		went forward by rail with nil command, N.R. R.2.o. and B. Leonard, R30. to Cont: of CANWNDHAM. nent with No 920 to get our forward offices from letter N39.	

WAR DIARY
or
INTELLIGENCE SUMMARY

(Erase heading not required.)

Army Form C. 2118

Place	Date	Hour	Summary of Events and Information	Remarks and references to Appendices
SAX-MUND-HAM	17/9/15		Examined Blanketing gear returning from IPSWICH and found it faulty. 1637	
	18/9/15		After inspection of 14th Batty Gun Park R.S.M. Horseman there and Cook Plume had some attention. The Cook Plumes were	
	19/9/15			
	20/9/15		Wing 2nd sd. concerning the excess Losses. 1637. Verbal orders to shift ourselves ready to leave b-Borden on 22nd inst. 6 Guns 355 Bis. M.T. Advance Party 1 Officer & 40 men cycle to Borden	
	21/9/15		's Officers and 90 other ranks arrived from 2/c ResR Bde A.P.D. Numerical distribution to-morrow received with	
	22/9/15			
BORDON	23/9/15		for b-Borden Bde and the remaining S. O.Rs. accompanied the M.T. Horses in the afternoon on 19th. Corp Smith (2) Lieut Ramsay and Lieut Whittall accompanying officers for forming up of 25 cases of Labs. 1637 Examining to date 1637 Examination of b-Borden by one Officer (N.S.) Bist: batty 1637	

Army Form C. 2118.

WAR DIARY
—or—
INTELLIGENCE SUMMARY.
(Erase heading not required.)

Instructions regarding War Diaries and Intelligence Summaries are contained in F. S. Regs., Part II. and the Staff Manual respectively. Title pages will be prepared in manuscript.

Hour, Date, Place	Summary of Events and Information	Remarks and references to Appendices
BORDON 25.9.15	Drawing Stores & equipment all day 1802	Oct 15
26.9.15	Continued yesterday's work. Shewmurd Lt Turp R.O. 9th Hrs. Bns. inspected the horses Inspection very severe. All horses were picketed as well. Have recently received Lieut Bromley & 76 infant soldiers in place of such Yeomanry and we are very short of N.C.O's with Yeomanry experience. All the signallers had passed but one who arrived with 2 Sergts on Special Duties. Inspected yesterday 1637	Dec '15
29.9.15	Kings inspection 16"Div Rehearsal on Mr Kells exercises 1737.	
29.9.15	Col Pratt Received Officers inspected horses	
30.9.15	Kings Review of 36 (Ulster) Division HANKLEY common 1637	

H.B. Tucker

36th Division

1/2nd London Bde: RFA.

Vol I

Col 15

CONFIDENTIAL

WAR DIARY

of

1/2 London Bde. RFA

from 1st Oct to 31st Oct 1915

Army Form C. 2118.

1/2nd Lanc. Bde R.F.A.

WAR DIARY
or
INTELLIGENCE SUMMARY.

(Erase heading not required.)

Instructions regarding War Diaries and Intelligence Summaries are contained in F. S. Regs., Part II. and the Staff Manual respectively. Title pages will be prepared in manuscript.

Place	Date	Hour	Summary of Events and Information	Remarks and references to Appendices
BORDON	1915 Oct. 2	3.45 P.M.	Left for SOUTHAMPTON embarking at LIPTHOOK. Remainder of Bde coming by later trains. All arrived without casualties.	
SOUTHAMPTON	3	7.0 a.m.	Commenced embarking on different ships. Headquarters of Bde on the "Duchess" Archam Brookhurst Line who also	
		7.0	everything for our transport.	
HARVE	4	9.30 a.m. 1.0 P.M.	Commenced disembarking and moved out to Rest Camp. Lies at 1.0 P.M.	
	5	10.30 a.m. 3.15 P.M. 1.30	Moved from Rest Camp 2 entrains. Train left.	
LONGEAU		6.10	Arrived, detrained and marched to AMIENS to VILLERS	
VILLERS BOCAGE		6.10	BOCAGE arriving at 6.10 P.M. Guns, Limbers and Horse Lines in various orchards — Officers & men in billets.	
	7		Went to FRESSELLES 36th Div H.Q. also Div Artey H.Q. Went to MORLIENS 108 (Fifty) R.F.A. with extremes inner granyd.	

WAR DIARY or INTELLIGENCE SUMMARY.

(Erase heading not required.)

Army Form C. 2118

1/2nd Lowland R.F.A.

Instructions regarding War Diaries and Intelligence Summaries are contained in F. S. Regs., Part II and the Staff Manual respectively. Title pages will be prepared in manuscript.

Place	Date	Hour	Summary of Events and Information	Remarks and references to Appendices
VILLERS BOCAGE	1915 Oct. 8		Received orders instructing us in arranging Relations & Forage for Divisional move. 1407	
		9.30 a.m.	A/2nd Lowland Battery received to THIEVRES when 9.30 a.m. Battery had Cickets 1407	
THIEVRES	10	6.30 a.m.	Left with RGs and went at small staff & billets at Bus-les-Artois for Q.Rs. hack on to SAILLY au BOIS. Having arranged for Billets & RJ then convoyed up into position. English and the horselines were arranged at THIEVRES 1407	
SAILLY au BOIS			Arranged & Supervised arrangements at THIEVRES 1407 At 9.30 p.m. 12 2nd Div. Battery moved on R. of the Battery — 8 wounded Farriers and most of the Men's Rations arrived near the battery 3 shell fell over the village	
	13		Battery opened fire at U.C.R.D as it was considered that the battery spent energy Gun-Bell before long teaching to about another enemy Gun-Bell before being the battery of 4 rounds — reply lasted about 1407 (2 shell fell over the village 1407)	

Army Form C. 2118

WAR DIARY
or
INTELLIGENCE SUMMARY.   1/2 Lon Bde R.F.A.

(Erase heading not required.)

Place	Date	Hour	Summary of Events and Information	Remarks and references to Appendices
BAILLY au BOIS	1915 Oct 14		Brig Genl Ross Johnston & Wrington CRAs of 48th & 36th Div inspected when the Batteries were firing. They considered considerable improvement is required & that the Batteries lack discipline & execution. Head Qrs at OP Ropes OO 22 8 of 48th Bde HQ.	
	15		Head k-wagon have found things better, but also found a few cases of Negligence in some of the Recruits. Stationed at BORDON HQ.	
	16		Genl Fanshaw GOC 48th Div & the CRA went round the Batteries and direct/have found to be improved & gun in course taken of cognizant. The sports frequently of the 3/10 Batty, had a most interesting & instructive talk with CO Belgian 1st Stand Bde RFA at HEBERTUNE HQ.	
	17		Village Shelled (about 150) had 2 wounded HQ.	
	18		Batteries fired 150 rounds, balance of their 100 rounds pr Batty, twenty led Practice reported "Sam" HQ.	

WAR DIARY
or
INTELLIGENCE SUMMARY.

Army Form C. 2118

1/2 2 Lon Bde R20

(Erase heading not required.)

Instructions regarding War Diaries and Intelligence Summaries are contained in F. S. Regs. Part II. and the Staff Manual respectively. Title pages will be prepared in manuscript.

Place	Date	Hour	Summary of Events and Information	Remarks and references to Appendices
SAILLY	19		Brig Gen Rom Islandin came here. Said the Battery had opened good & heard well. Sent one of his Offrs to instruct the Battery. Returned to THIEVRES after dusk. MD	
THIEVRES	20		Battery returned to VILLERS BOCAGE in the morning. Brig Sec. Called for orders in the afternoon & wished to remain Horse lines Sent Bty to ... MD	
VILLERS BOCAGE	21		Summoned Division. Found difficulty in ascertaining whereof the Division & then putting off Tps See Report. Forwarded and an unfortunate & surprising night at the house. Ordered and an unfortunate & surprising night at the house. Our own troops panicked at the sound of our own guns & flew eastwards in disorder to battle at BONNEVILLE. Found that troops had left town in a very bad state. MD	
BONNEVILLE	22		Went into billet at BERNIE. R&K Billets somewhere having partly lost precious troops. Difficulty in getting billets for Officers & last were but I war to ... Surrage MD	

WAR DIARY
or
INTELLIGENCE SUMMARY.
(Erase heading not required.)

Army Form C. 2118
1/2 Z Hors Bde R.F.A.

Place	Date	Hour	Summary of Events and Information	Remarks and references to Appendices
BERNUIL	1915 Feb 23		Batteries had a reed day for cleaning up and trying to get Billets & Horse lines in better condition. The CRA came had a look round in the early afternoon. AAA	
	24		Sunday Church Parades. Gen J. Munton Comdg CRA & Lt Col CRA inspected Gun Park & Horse lines. Found too much of one Gun detailed or detached with any Horses not likely to get into condition soon to include City Hors. AAA Spoke particularly of the great importance of keeping Ammunition in hourly equally Temperature. Found it from beginning good. But Gun & Limber fairly well but Great care would be taken with the Ammunition to get placed more immediately before a later supply is finished. AAA	
	25		The Batteries went to Bernaven twice on Exercise Every E. along AMIENS — DOULLENS road which the Kings and the President of the French Republic passed in motors AAA Our Roty Tactical Exercise. Some ground brought light	
	26			

Army Form C. 2118

WAR DIARY
or
INTELLIGENCE SUMMARY.

(Erase heading not required.)

Place	Date	Hour	Summary of Events and Information	Remarks and references to Appendices

BERNEVAL

Amputation

From 36 DIV
To 38 DIV (4.12.15)

War Diary

of

1/2 London Brigade R.F.A.

from 1st Nov. 1915 to 30th Nov. 1915

36/47
56

1/2 London Bble R.F.U.
Nov Dec. 9 Jany ——— 8 v 11

56 —

36 ½ —
to 38 ¼ —
11.12.15.

Army Form C. 2118.

1/2 Lon. Bde. R.F.A.

WAR DIARY
or
INTELLIGENCE SUMMARY.
(Erase heading not required.)

Instructions regarding War Diaries and Intelligence Summaries are contained in F. S. Regs., Part II. and the Staff Manual respectively. Title pages will be prepared in manuscript.

Place	Date	Hour	Summary of Events and Information	Remarks and references to Appendices
BERNEUIL	1915 Nov 1		Wet all day, and brewing much interrupted. Inspected Billets again and lost was all 4 weeks arrears letter arrangement to 4th Batty HQ?	
	2		Fifty Bde Jackal Field Day. Heavy rain all the time this was reclamation day and several points found out. Telephones HQ?	
	3		Covered with Bde Breezed? Ammunition supply scheme HQ? Brigade Field Day to test communication and men had been on the lookout from the supposed enemys locations HQ?	
	4		Reviewed of Arty Field Day. Infantry very noisy. Found it extremely difficult to understand. Stores and HE? had diff- iculty in making position of our Batty HQ?	
	5		G.O.B.S. inspected the horses. Appeared satisfied.	
	6		Reconnaissance area for 8th Field Day was much the same the ground occupied on 5th inst. HQ?	

WAR DIARY
INTELLIGENCE SUMMARY

(Erase heading not required.)

Army Form C. 2118.

LIEUT.-COLONEL
COMMANDING 1/24 LONDON REGT.

Instructions regarding War Diaries and Intelligence Summaries are contained in F.S. Regs., Part II. and the Staff Manual respectively. Title pages will be prepared in manuscript.

Place	Date	Hour	Summary of Events and Information	Remarks and references to Appendices
BERNEVAL			*[handwritten entries, largely illegible]*	

Army Form C. 2118.

WAR DIARY
or
INTELLIGENCE SUMMARY.

(Erase heading not required.)

LIEUT.-COLONEL
COMMANDING 1/2ND LON{D.?} ...

Instructions regarding War Diaries and Intelligence Summaries are contained in F. S. Regs., Part II and the Staff Manual respectively. Title pages will be prepared in manuscript.

Place	Date	Hour	Summary of Events and Information	Remarks and references to Appendices
BERMEUL	1915 Dec. 13		Reconnoitred ground for Reduisdoups Bty Bay found some difficult positions. O.C. Barker and advised at [?] preparing Billeting Movisions for load execution. 1837.	
	14		Worked several I. sec and could be done to improve Billets and Horse Shelters for the winter. Went to see the C.R.A. with R.E.s to Subcommanding for Icconnois 1937.	
	15		Inspected Field Bays under the C.R.A. Positions occupied were considered good and intercommunication between bats were generally good. Communication though by tel up from H.Q. to the Batty position where were to R.E. lines to should be communication from Rgy. N____ position in service section as Batty are exposed with extremely Bad Screen road though. Lunch Groomers & 215 throates were Burrows reported being attacked for instruction. Reconnoissance to 28 received of 1837. Met C.R.A. and saw positions allotted by Batteries	
	16			
	17			

Army Form C. 2118.

WAR DIARY
or
INTELLIGENCE SUMMARY.
(Erase heading not required)

Instructions regarding War Diaries and Intelligence
Summaries are contained in F. S. Regs. Part II.
and the Staff Manual respectively. Title pages
will be prepared in manuscript.

Place	Date 1918 June	Hour	Summary of Events and Information	Remarks and references to Appendices
BERNEUIL				
	18		For Routine Returns with R.E. & R.A.S. See orderly room records of the weather. Received information that L/Corp L S Douglens transferred from York Depôt from 16th May. Power Keeper to R.A. Place. 1917. L/Cpl F. A. Faber left at 11.30 am	
	19		Capt Drummond RAM here stated that W. Macdonald died 15 May stating he will probably be sent home on Wednesday May 17 to take command.	
	20		L.R.A. Inspected 3 aerial arrival N field and August hour standing J. Work delayed owing to have hung to wait 3 cuts re from R.E. 9. L. # Rd.	
	22		Co-operation with Command R.A. Portage R.A. W.O. 16 Sec L. 30 L.A.C. Section has that applied for Smiths & W. G. Leakey B.C.O. Lt A.C. Section with Platoons Capt. Mcgaw SM Askam M.C. Green	
	23rd 2.45		Lieut-Colonel C Macdonnell joined for duty.	

WAR DIARY
or
INTELLIGENCE SUMMARY.

(Erase heading not required.)

Army Form C. 2118.

Place	Date	Hour	Summary of Events and Information	Remarks and references to Appendices
BERNEUIL	24th		CO's inspection 1/6 Battery	
	25th		1/6 Battery moved from BERNEUIL to HAVERNAS. 1st duty with artillery School. CO inspection 1/5 Batterys	
	26th			
	27th		CO's inspection 1/4 Battery and Brigade Ammunition Column	
	28th			
	29th		Brigade (less 1/6 Battery) proceeded by route march to FRANQUEVILLE	

WAR DIARY
or
INTELLIGENCE SUMMARY.
(Erase heading not required.)

Army Form C. 2118.

Instructions regarding War Diaries and Intelligence Summaries are contained in F.S. Regs., Part II. and the Staff Manual respectively. Title pages will be prepared in manuscript.

Place	Date	Hour	Summary of Events and Information	Remarks and references to Appendices
FIENVILL	1	11.15	Sat forth 9 AM to ascertain units mostly in field + what it. We knew of it situated. Roads to be in after field in groups of men. Used jitney known in a roll if possible. but were Muslim remorse to lived into withdraw every load + no doubt are about the night.	
	2		Set forth 9 AM for South Angels. Went round 10 of Infantry brigade units (illeg) together through the villages of RIBEAUCOURT and PERNAVILLERS FIENVILLERS & [illeg] had a lively day met with Cdr (illeg) 2 Infm (illeg) from their trades. Arrived AFA W.E. Red man. (illeg) till a Cople and we [illeg] only [illeg] for [illeg].	
	3	11.15	Went to round lines. (illeg) infantry 4th Bg home and left to duty. Programme here fairly not long [illeg] we was one [illeg] the battery very fines but did not ready so men + battery no day a home. Started Sagum and to ST HILAIRE 1 AM. men find it in ground though there from 16 looking well. 1 arrived then let a new life very little orderly. Had lunch infantry at [illeg] (illeg) have at BERMENIL [illeg] (illeg). Very black news [illeg] still very full + trace the roads still very fine.	

2111 W.W.V.&S. 74341 750.000 3/15 D. D. & L. A.D.S.S./FormsC 2118.

WAR DIARY
or
INTELLIGENCE SUMMARY

Army Form C. 2118.

Place	Date	Hour	Summary of Events and Information	Remarks and references to Appendices
BERNEUIL	5/11/15		Officers of 20. infantry 5th Batty, horse, the same had with considerable interest in the Batty went round the Batty horse in horse lines.	
"	6/11/15		A.D.V.S. inspected 1/1st London Amb. horse 10 A.M. remarks that they compare very favourably with other Amb.; examined and 2 horses to M. Lucie's latter all cases of Sweetie. Inspected horses of 6.S.S. Dragoons at St. HILAIRE. also went from here to HOUDENCOURT to see horses of 108. Field Ambulance latter think horses very favourable. Sent 2 horses in float to M. Lucie we had one (Chronic Dermatitis, 2:30 P.M. inspected horses of Head Quarters all of which on looking very well.	
"	7/11/15	10:30 AM	After rist paraded infantry 4th Batty horse + rain they all show much improvement. At 2:30 P.M. inspected 5th By horses which also have improved even they no doubt feel I was 15 room suspicious many sound hind quarters of this type. This major + warley first formed opinion due to still a gradually developing	
"	8/11/15		Sit paraded as usual. 10 AM went from FIENVILLIERS. BERNAVILLE VACQUERIE + THIEBAUCOURT under air flour mechant Lan francais, on rid. Lam. only 4 came out of 209 animals (horses + mules) 2.30 P.M. went round to S.+ A. Column lines, the latter in an awful state owing to weather	
	9/11/15			
	10/11/15			

WAR DIARY
or
INTELLIGENCE SUMMARY.

Army Form C. 2118.

Place	Date	Hour	Summary of Events and Information	Remarks and references to Appendices
BEAUVAL	11/11/15			
"	12/11/15	10.30 A.M.	went HOUDENCOURT & then to ST HILAIRE. the horses all looked well on it.	
			Luckily the bad weather has caused our Cavalry duty in front of the Commandant's Quarters recommenced and so it costs feed like in time to prevent this.	
"	13/11/15		August 10.30 A.M. all horses in Divisional Column still take up much all the morn. afternoon & evening round Battalion & finally stable to feed and horses in of the Divisional Column.	
"	14/11/15		Routine duties with Brigade.	
"	15/11/15	2.30 P.M.	went FIENVILLERS. Inspected 2nd B. LANCASHIRE FUSILIERS. then home early which will eventually they have been in trans' areas during of War.	
"	16/11/15		visited BERNAVILLE. RIBEAUCOURT. HOUDENCOURT. FRASU. met Lieut. all the units have very few sick horses. O/C FRASU at whom the LO.D thinks Cuthbert have in settled in a bag from good health. 25 Remounts arrived for 2nd Garden Brigade thought some of horses very poor but many very very poor lot. there few w. Bates' come in from everyone very hard to the due to shelling but result some horses with Bastin shoulder fails not	
	17/11/15			

WAR DIARY
or
INTELLIGENCE SUMMARY.

Army Form C. 2118.

Place	Date	Hour	Summary of Events and Information	Remarks and references to Appendices
BERNEUIL	14/11/15		in sufficient shelter, mules & wagons not what not billed until 19th. Found much shell supplied & shelter defective	
	15/11/15	9AM	Sick parade 9AM @ 10AM avoided b.c in detail whig - Remainder to various Units. Some of the Remainder were sum Stah round that quarters still 11AM were ST. HILAIRE visit Dragon Squadron motor m/g to road here	
	19/11/15		G.C by M.O. to take specialist in Town Major of DOULLONS, our way to the Brigade, as could not arrange with b.c. Destroyed horse with syphin Arthritis & elfort for by order of ADVS. PM returned fettled practice & exercise quite increased & exercise of ambulance of faits continue	
	20/11/15		Inspected all horses No 3 Calvalry Division at Albain. Reported as usually sound fitting. Leave & DVS arrived of which now Canadian	
			ADVS inspected sit down afront this have husky, all ail horse men of farrier his Canada on monthly 6 duty, from BERNEVIL went with ADVS CHOISEN UIR	
	28/11/15		& FRASEN inspect 10 & 4 LW Ambulance.	
	23/11/15		After sail parade of EBERNAVILLE to see horses D.A. Column sent & home from here M Leboi, on a case of fruitned road horse reward by thieves of flew fleas mind & FIENVILLERS inspect 2 Bn LANC FUSILIERS for him the unit could 2353 Wt. W5.11/1436 500,000 3/15 D. D. & L. A.D.S.S./Forms/C.2118. in charge of M Small. By order of ADVS.	

WAR DIARY
INTELLIGENCE SUMMARY.

Army Form C. 2118.

(Erase heading not required.)

Instructions regarding War Diaries and Intelligence Summaries are contained in F. S. Regs., Part II. and the Staff Manual respectively. Title pages will be prepared in manuscript.

Place	Date	Hour	Summary of Events and Information	Remarks and references to Appendices
GENEUIL	25/11/15		The first wounded arrived this dressing station about 5th By team might shot up truck from HDUS to HOUDENCOURT. The two Impedes were had 35kg yesterday in front of 10th Fld Amb.	
	26/11/15		Had great success with B. Cpt F. HAYENAS, very sorry to lose time to bring tea but battery of the Bngd. 10AM ADVS removed to HOUDENCOURT into 2 Officers Mess huts. Lt. Yelverton to pick ammunition tins. Day the old time setting down work & supply of drugs to field dressing stations. Capt. Olde about 3 hrs into 10M HAves had Ford moved that ST HILAIRE Dressn station had my truck very taxing to land out though portable kits. My boss night For flux former ambulance at HOUD-	
	27/11/15		ENCOURT for two hours as no better. A Dus sent round to Lines (the two ARel methods Of note the very important hops HOUDENCOURT and HDUS the rest Ap.	
	28/11/15		ST HILAIRE by others DERNEVIL & FRANDEVILLE 2.30 PM & ERUME aPMon evin ley Capt. Allen. Came the day about next to 9:30 and attle; to carry for for dressing Stn.	
FRANDE- VILLE	30/11/15		GnFRANA (William Midday) Geneuil Sally	

A.D.S.S./Forms/C. 2118.

SDN ATTACHED 38th (DC of) 1/2nd LONDON BRIGADE R.F.A.
From 3.5 to 11.12.15 3.1.16.
Vol 2A

Army Form C. 2118.

WAR DIARY
or
INTELLIGENCE SUMMARY
(Erase heading not required.)

Place	Date	Hour	Summary of Events and Information	Remarks and references to Appendices
FRANQUEVILLE	DEC 4		5 horses destroyed owing to Glanders	
	5		All horses 4th, 5th & Brigade Headquarters destroyed. 6th Battery relieved from duty with Artillery School HAVERNAS and arrived by route march BARLETTE.	2332
	6		All horses 6th Battery & Brigade Ammunition Column destroyed.	
	8		1 horse destroyed owing to Glanders	
	10		Brigade transferred from 36th (Ulster) Division to 31st (W&L) Division and 3 batteries Brigade Ammunition Column & Headquarters entrained at PONTRÉMY (3 trains)	
PONTRÉMY	11		Detrained 4th Battery & 5th Battery Holgts & Bde Ammunition Column at THIENNES proceeded by route march to BOESEGHEM. Detrained 6th Battery & ½ 5th Battery at AIRE proceeded by route march to BOESEGHEM. Weather had a condition of entraining & detraining extremely difficult.	
BOESEGHEM	12			
	13		Inspection & final allotment of billets at BOESEGHEM.	
	14		Received orders attachment GUARDS DIVISIONAL ARTILLERY for a period	

WAR DIARY
or
INTELLIGENCE SUMMARY.

Army Form C. 2118.

(Erase heading not required.)

Instructions regarding War Diaries and Intelligence Summaries are contained in F. S. Regs., Part II and the Staff Manual respectively. Title pages will be prepared in manuscript.

Place	Date	Hour	Summary of Events and Information	Remarks and references to Appendices
BERGUIN	20		Brigade marched to NEUF BERQUIN via MERVILLE (LE SART) and 3rd and 4th batteries & Bde. Amm. Column marched to LA GORGUE	
			Wagon Lines established on LA GORGUE – ESTAIRES – SAILLY road	
LAVENTIE	21		Headquarters moved to LAVENTIE.	
	22		Gunners reporting for Bn. moved to billets in vicinity of gun pits. Work started on these.	
	23		Old Gun pits of Battery brought up into emplacements vacant to established. 4th Battery registered with this single gun.	
	24		Battery pulled in all gun pits. 4th Batt^y near LAVENTIE	
			5th " " ROUGE CROIX. LA BASSÉ road	
			6th " " HOUGEMONT REDOUBT	
			RUE BACQUEROT	
	25		4th & 5th batteries and isolated 1st Battery in action at the following points 4th Battery near LAVENTIE. 5th Battery ROUGE CROIX. 1st Battery HOUGEMONT REDOUBT near FAUQUISSART	
	26		Work continued on gun pits by all batteries.	

Army Form C. 2118.

WAR DIARY
or
INTELLIGENCE SUMMARY.
(Erase heading not required.)

Place	Date	Hour	Summary of Events and Information	Remarks and references to Appendices
LAVENTIE			4th Battery registration & retaliation	
			5th " registered, 1 section 6th Battery registered	
	29		4th & 5th Batterys registered	
			1 section 6th Battery withdrawn to wagon line	
			Received orders to join 4th Corps.	
	30		All guns withdrawn to wagon line	
			Operations & bombardment of enemys strong post in which	
			4th Battery was to take part (100 rds H.E.) postponed until	
			31st Dec. owing to mist.	

ATTACHED 47 DIV

1-2ND LONDON BRIGADE RFA
JAN-FEB 1916

Army Form C. 2118.

WAR DIARY
or
INTELLIGENCE SUMMARY.
(Erase heading not required.)

47th (from 3rd = 31.1.16.
1/9th LONDON BRIGADE RFA VIIA

Place	Date	Hour	Summary of Events and Information JANUARY 1916	Remarks and references to Appendices
LAVENTIE	DEC. 31			
LIERES.	JAN 3		The brigade marched from the wagon line at LA GORGUE via LILLERS to LIERES where it was billeted for the night.	
			Brigade inspected by Brig Gen Budworth G.O.C. IV Corps R.A. who expressed himself extremely pleased with the appearance of men & horses & their steadiness on parade	
	4		Notification received that the Brigade would form part of the IV Corps Counter Battery Group	
VERQUIN	5		Brigade preceded by Junior march to VERQUIN where Brigade (own Column) & Batteries wagon line to be stationed Brigade Headquarters	
PHILOSOPHE 6.			moved into NAZINGARBE BREWERY. 1 section 5th Battery moved into action in VERMELLES 1 section 5th Battery moved into action in LENS	
NAZINGARBE BREWERY				
	8		BETHUNE and near FOSSE 7. 1 section of 5th & 4th Batteries in action	
	10		5th Battery heavily shelled. 1 direct hit on emplacement.	

WAR DIARY or INTELLIGENCE SUMMARY.

Army Form C. 2118.

1/2nd LONDON BRIGADE R.F.A.

Place	Date	Hour	Summary of Events and Information	Remarks and references to Appendices
MAZINGARBE	11		One gun b½ Battery came into action in QUALITY STREET FOSSE 7	
	16		Two guns b½ Battery moved up	
	18		One gun b½ Battery moved up	
	19		One gun b½ Battery moved up	
			All actions from this date onward were daily engaged against enemy batteries & towards HULLUCH, BOIS HUGO, HILL 70, CITES St AUGUSTE, St PIERRE St LAURENT St EDOUARD St JEAN DAR and LENS. Gun OPS were in the trenches between N of LOOS. VI Brigade is attached to the POOLE Heavy group to cover B½ Battery itself and the Brigade zone extends from HAISNES in the N to LEVIN in the S.	
	21st		B½ Battery "Gun" barely shelled by enemy's 5.9 from the direction of DOUVRIN. Two guns hit, two men wounded (both slightly). Battery temporarily silenced as position had to be evacuated. Enemy fired on position from 11.30 am to 3.30 pm about 150 rounds high explosive, & without damaged guns withdrawn to wagon line	

WAR DIARY
or
INTELLIGENCE SUMMARY.

(Erase heading not required.)

1/2nd LONDON Army Form C. 2118.
BRIGADE R.F.A.

Place	Date	Hour	Summary of Events and Information	Remarks and references to Appendices
MAZINGARBE	Dec 27th		From the nature of position occupied by 5th Battery this battery was daily subjected to an intermittent fire from 4.2 Hows & 5.9 Hows, mainly from the direction of DOUVRIN & METALLURGIQUE (enfilade)	
	28th		The battery fired 796 rounds HE. Considerable artillery activity	
	29th		The battery fired 730 rounds HE. Considerable artillery activity. 5th Battery shelled with gas shells (44) lachrymose, no damage done.	
	30th		5th Battery has night-section again in action battery in position under roadway to FOSSE 7. N of Quality Street.	
	31st		Heavy bombardment on enemy trenches which provoked little retaliation.	

[signature]

LIEUT-COLONEL
COMMANDING 1/2 LONDON BDE R.F.A.

47th (Lossie?) 25.2.16.

SDN
25.2.16

II/2nd Lon. Bde. RFA.

War Diary
for
Month of Feby 1916

Vol III

WAR DIARY or INTELLIGENCE SUMMARY

Army Form C. 2118.

1/2 LONDON BRIGADE R F A

FEBRUARY 1916

Place	Date	Hour	Summary of Events and Information	Remarks and references to Appendices
MAZINGARBE	1st 2nd		Our batteries heavily shelled from direction of METALURGIQUE. New positions reconnoitred close to the VERMELLES-GRENAY Railway Line.	
	5th		During the past week the 4th battery at VERMELLES and the 6th battery at QUALITY STREET were frequently shelled with a high velocity armour piercing shell, silent in flight and bursting with a considerable noise.	
	8th		From this morning the enemy's artillery fire appears to be slackening on the gun positions	
	12th		4th & 6th Batteries changed positions	
	14th		Battery going to QUALITY STREET, 6th Battery to VERMELLES. The front is still quiet as far as our battery positions are concerned	
	17th		BRIGADE HQRS, BATTERIES & B.A.C. withdrawn from line & proceed by route march to MARLES-LEZ-MINES	
MARLES	18th		BRIGADE billeted at MARLES	

Army Form C. 2118.

WAR DIARY
or
INTELLIGENCE SUMMARY.

(Erase heading not required.)

Instructions regarding War Diaries and Intelligence Summaries are contained in F. S. Regs., Part II. and the Staff Manual respectively. Title pages will be prepared in manuscript.

Place	Date	Hour	Summary of Events and Information	Remarks and references to Appendices
MARLES	19"		Letter received from Col Poole commanding IV Corps Counter Batt. Group, & GOC 47th Division complimenting the 2n London Brigade on their behaviour while in action around LOOS — True copies attached	
			 (Map to illustrate) by N.M.F.S.	
ALLAIN?			From ? hence Laird MARLES LES MINES & entrained for PONT REMY	
AUX? 20"			Left & St. INVERTIN arrived at PONT REMY 12.15 p.m.	
			Marched arrived ? ? ? ? ? ? & Batty.	
			Harry had instructions to march at PONT REMY from 11am to 1pm. Officers & Men had uncommon rest at ? ? got at station.	
	26"		Orders when return ? for & got at station.	
			? and first	
			? Officers luck invited at Lunch in Col Watts?	
			? regimental dining ? assemble. Very enjoyable	
NETHUNE 27"			? ? ? ? ? ? 2 ? with 163rd Brigade Corners Batt.	

R.T. Lewis?
LC Comdg? RG?

Col. Poole
    Commanding Council Battery Group.

    The G.O.C 47th (London) Division directs me to convey to you his appreciation of the support given by the batteries under your command whenever occasion has arisen.

    The calls for this support have, he his aware, been frequent and at times difficult to comply with, owing to various circumstances, but it has been noticeable how rapidly it has been forthcoming under all conditions. He trusts that the excellent understanding existing between this Division & the batteries under your command will continue.

    He would be obliged if you would communicate his appreciation to all ranks under your command.

G/750/9   Lieut Colonel
14.2.16   General Staff,
                                 47th (London) Division.

½ London Brigade R.F.A.
        For information and communication to all concerned

15.2.16   Certified true copy

B.E.F
18th Feb 16

My dear Macdonell,

I was so sorry to miss you last night but I have got a most beastly cold which knocked me up.

I wanted to take the opportunity of thanking you and all your officers for the capital work you have done with the C.B. group. I feel indebted to you + all your officers for the constant cheerful co-operation under what were sometimes very trying circumstances.

General Budworth tells me he has taken steps to thank you specially so I hope you will hear in due course.

I wish the very best of luck to you and all the company, + I hope we shall soon be working together again.

Yours Sincerely

(Signed) F. A. Poole
Lt Col Commanding
IV Corps Counter Battery Group

Certified true copy
Macdonell
Lt Col

Copy.

IV Corps No 7794/A.
IV Corps Arty No 274/146.

IV Corps.

The 1st London Divisional Artillery — The three (3) 18 pdr Brigades of this Artillery have all, at different periods between 7th January and 17th February, 1916, been in action on the IVth Corps front. They have assisted in Counter Battery and Divisional Artillery work.

The work at all times and under all circumstances has been efficiently and cheerfully performed. The conduct of all ranks has been excellent.

The above Artillery has not had any previous extended experience in action, and their conduct and work is deserving of commendation.

H.Q. IVth Corps Arty.   (Sd) C.E.D. Budworth, Brig.-Genl.
18.2.16.   G.O.C. R.A. IVth Corps.

2.

Headquarters.
1st Corps.

Forwarded for your information.
I gladly endorse the favourable report made by General Budworth.

    (Sd) Henry Wilson
21st February, 1916.   Lieutenant General.
    Commanding IVth Corps.

3.

Headquarters.
1st Division.

Forwarded for your information and communication to the G.O.C. 1st London Divisional Artillery.

    (Sd) C.G. Maude,
1st C.H.Q.   Captain.
22/2/16.   D.A.A. + Q.M.G. 1st Corps.

16th Div. No 6477/G 16.

4.

London Divisional Arty.

In forwarding this report to you for your retention I must express on behalf of the 16th Division our regret at losing the services of your efficient brigade, and my own regret at losing the Brigadier and his staff.

(Sd) W.B Hickie.
Maj. Gen.
Commdg 16th Irish Division.

25.2.16.

5.

Officer Commanding
1/2nd London Brigade R.F.A.

For your information and communication to unit commanders.

The C.R.A. desires me to say that he is well satisfied with this report and that it reflects great credit on all concerned.

(Sd) W.J. McJay. Major.
Brigade Major R.A
56th Division.

28.2.16.

6.

O.C. Units.

Certified true copy

[signature]
CAPTAIN, R.F.A. T.F.
ADJUTANT 3/2ND LONDON BRIGADE, R.F.A.

29.2.16.

56

12nd London Bde R.F.A.

WAR DIARY for March 1916

Vol IV

2nd LONDON BRIGADE R.F.A.

Army Form C. 2118

WAR DIARY or INTELLIGENCE SUMMARY

MARCH

(Stamped: 2nd LONDON BRIGADE ROYAL FIELD ARTILLERY 30 MAR 1916)

Place	Date	Hour	Summary of Events and Information	Remarks and references to Appendices
L'ETOILE	FEB 26		Brigade billeted at L'ETOILE in 168th Inf Brigade area. Batteries recruiting & rapidly training advance parties and guns and in units.	
	MARCH 1st to 11th		O.C. recovered from leave in England.	
	7th		Brigade proceeded by route march with 168th Inf Brigade to CANDAS & there billeted. Major Adam left for England (15th)	
CANDAS	12th		Brigade proceeded by route march with 168th Inf Brigade to BERTRANCOURT & there billeted	
BERTRANCOURT			Wires picketed in the open till front line reclining & instructed with successful work by all units.	
	31st		R. Shoyne Artillery Group command B officers (4 inf.) 168th Brigade attached for instruction.	
			Major Chapman 9th South Staffs Regt. O.C. the relief of the battery Capt'n Montgomerie in command of B Battery who carry out practical exercises with 168th Inf Brigade (London Scottish)	

2nd LONDON Brigade RFA

WAR DIARY
or
INTELLIGENCE SUMMARY.

Army Form C. 2118.

(Erase heading not required.)

MARCH

Place	Date	Hour	Summary of Events and Information	Remarks and references to Appendices
BERLEN COURT.	MARCH 28th 29th 30th		Permanent horse standings commenced by Brigade Ammunition Column. Tactical exercises with 4th Battery. Second course of instruction Artillery & Infantry officers commenced. Officers of the Brigade attended a display of Trench mortars and bombing at MANIN. The Commander-in-Chief and Lord Kitchener were present	

C. Macdonald
LIEUT.-COLONEL
COMMANDING 1/2ND LONDON BDE. R.F.A.

[Stamp: 2nd LONDON BRIGADE FIELD ARTILLERY 30 MAR. 1916]

WAR DIARY - Month of April 1916

Vol V

WAR DIARY or INTELLIGENCE SUMMARY

Army Form C. 2118.

APRIL 1916

1/2 LONDON BRIGADE ROYAL FIELD ARTILLERY

Place	Date	Hour	Summary of Events and Information	Remarks and references to Appendices
SECLIN CUFT	MARCH 31st		Battery & Brigade Training continued daily	
	APRIL 6		War Establishment of Brigade by General Paget GOC RA VI Corps.	
	7		Captain Lee assumed command of B/15 Battery.	
			C. Randall appointed to act as Adjutant.	
	15		104 Battery RFA joined the Brigade (4.5 in howitzer RFA)	
	17		2nd Lieut S. Mahin joined 46th Bde RFA at ARRAS on instruction.	
	19		Lieut Col Exelved B/ Battery & Lt Smith GIVENCHY LE NOBLE	
	21		104 Battery RFA carried out experiments in French gas mask. Lieut E. CAURDY to hospital.	
	23		2nd Lieut Greenwood (RHA) & Macdonell at Hull School Gunnery entered at St Pol	

Army Form C. 2118.

WAR DIARY
or
INTELLIGENCE SUMMARY 1/2 LONDON BRIGADE R.F.A.
(Erase heading not required.)

APRIL 1916

Instructions regarding War Diaries and Intelligence Summaries are contained in F. S. Regs., Part II. and the Staff Manual respectively. Title Pages will be prepared in manuscript.

Place	Date	Hour	Summary of Events and Information	Remarks and references to Appendices
BERLES au BOIS			4th Battery in conjunction with LONDON SCOTTISH carried out Stunt under BRIG GEN LOCH CMG. MAJOR ASCHWANDEN assumed command of 4th Battery on return from ENGLAND. MAJOR JACKSON proceeded to Saint Pheus until return at ST POL. 15 minute constant work was carried out nearly every hill making trench standings & general repairs was going on. All batteries continual wiring & driving exercises.	

[Stamp: 2/2 LONDON BRIGADE ROYAL FIELD ARTILLERY 30 APR 1916]

[Signature]
LIEUT-COLONEL
COMMANDING 2/2ND LONDON BDE RFA

281st. Brigade R.F.A.
late 1/2 London Bde R.F.A.
War Diary from 1st May
to 30th 1916

WAR DIARY or INTELLIGENCE SUMMARY

Army Form C. 2118.

1/2 London Brigade RFA
281 Brigade RFA

MAY 1916

Place	Date	Hour	Summary of Events and Information	Remarks and references to Appendices
BERLENCOURT	1		Big fire took place in 4th Battery billets, clothing & equipment of one section burnt.	
	3		109th Battery RFA inspected by OC Brigade. Captain RTJ Re resumed the duties of Adjutant	
SAILLY & PAS	6		Headquarters of Brigade moved in the line at SAILLY LE BOIS, all batteries and column proceeded by route march to PAS where winter line was established in canvas huts	
	7		4, 5, 6, & 109 batteries moved into line taking over from S Midland Brigade RFA all battery positions in the vicinity SAILLY- HEBUTERNE	Appendix A
	8		4, 5, 6, & 109 batteries completed registration of their Zones Artillery Group formed by the addition of the 105 London (Howitzer) Battery. Headquarters of the group at SAILLY. Front covered from GOMMECOURT WOOD to SUNKEN ROAD E of HEBUTERNE	
	9		Registration of all batteries continued. All batteries employed in improving & repairing battery positions and Telephone communications	

2449 Wt. W14957/M90 750,000 1/16 J.B.C. & A. Forms/C.2118/12.

Army Form C. 2118.

WAR DIARY or INTELLIGENCE SUMMARY

2nd London Brigade RFA TF
now 281 Brigade RFA

(Erase heading not required.)

MAY 1916

Place	Date	Hour	Summary of Events and Information	Remarks and references to Appendices
AILLY	12		Name of Brigade changed to 281 Brigade, RFA and batteries lettered as follows 4th = A battery, 5th = B battery, 6th = C battery, 109 = D battery, 10th London (How) Battery becomes A battery 263 Brigade.	
	13		One extra officer (Subaltern) added to establishment of the Brigade.	
	15/16	12.25 am	Intense & violent bombardment opened by enemy on our trenches infront of HEBUTERNE + S of Sunken Road (48 Divisional Sector) firing by salvos 59s, 42s = 77mm	
		12.30 am	All batteries of group in action on enemy's front trenches (at 1 per 1 round per gun 30 secs) fire effective & accurate, later the enemy's fire directed on communication trenches, barrage established on roads approaching HEBUTERNE, and on C battery position 77mm, later the enemy's bombardment died down and at 3.30 am it had entirely ceased	

Army Form C. 2118.

WAR DIARY
or
INTELLIGENCE SUMMARY
(Erase heading not required.)

281. Brigade RFA
(late 1/2. LONDON Brigade)

MAY 1916

Place	Date	Hour	Summary of Events and Information	Remarks and references to Appendices
SAILLY	16	9 am	b"/C/ Battery position heavily shelled with 5.9. about 150 shells	
		11 am	b"/C/ Battery again heavily shelled. Position had to be evacuated	
		to 11.45 am	no casualties. One gun hit, gun pits & dugouts much damaged. Battery intermittently shelled during the day. Battery withdrew from position & came into action on Sailly- Hebuterne Road, near SAILLY. Lt NATHAN, Bty Sergt major BUSH, Sergt BATH did great work, a displayed great bravery both whilst the battery was being shelled & in the retirement.	Appendix 1/2
	17		" Condition of front normal. All batteries continue registration	
	to			
	24		"	
	25		Divisional Operations commenced	

Army Form C. 2118.

WAR DIARY
or
INTELLIGENCE SUMMARY

281 Brigade RFA

MAY 1916

(Erase heading not required.)

Instructions regarding War Diaries and Intelligence Summaries are contained in F. S. Regs., Part II and the Staff Manual respectively. Title Pages will be prepared in manuscript.

Place	Date	Hour	Summary of Events and Information	Remarks and references to Appendices
HEBUTERNE	26th	10 pm	167th Inf Brigade commenced to dig the new trench, approximately 800 yards in front of our present line	Appendix B
		6	167th Inf Brigade withdrew to front trenches & there	
		1.30 am	HEBUTERNE - SAILLY the night passed comparatively quietly little shelling or machine gun fire	
			Day passed quietly	
	27th	10 pm	167th Inf Brigade continued operations in front of our line	
	27th	6	that part of night passed quietly, but enemy appeared nervous at times and fired sharp bursts of fire (77 m/m on our front & support lines & communication trenches on guns retaliated	
		1.30 am	dealing with certain points & batteries this retaliation proved most satisfactory in checking fire, minenwerfer & machine guns were also dealt with by our 18 pdrs. 4.5 & 6" Hows	
		1 am later	the enemy's fire on our wiring parties became more intense causing many casualties	

WAR DIARY
or
INTELLIGENCE SUMMARY

281 Brigade RFA

Army Form C. 2118

MAY

Place	Date	Hour	Summary of Events and Information	Remarks and references to Appendices
SAILLY	28/29	1.30	167th Inf Brigade withdrew to SOUASTRE. Complimentary telegrams & letters received from Major Gen Snow commanding VII Corps & Gen Nugent. 167 Inf Brigade	Appendices C & D

Mackworth
LIEUT-COLONEL
COMMANDING 281 Bde RFA

SECRET.

RELIEF OF 48th DIVISIONAL ARTILLERY BY 56th
DIVISIONAL ARTILLERY:

Reference Map
1/20,000
57 D,N.E.

Copy No. 2

OPERATION ORDER No.2.

BY BRIGADIER GENERAL R.J.G.ELKINGTON, C. M. G.

COMMANDING 56th DIVISIONAL ROYAL ARTILLERY.

6th May 1916.

1. The 56th Divisional Artillery will relieve the 48th Divisional Artillery as shewn in attached table, on the night of the 7/8 and 9/10th May. Details to be arranged between Group Commanders.

2. No vehicle will pass through SAILLY before 8-15 p.m. on either night.

3. Ammunition dumped with guns will be handed over by 48th Division Batteries to incoming Batteries, an equivalent amount being handed over by 56th Divisional Ammunition Column to 48th Divisional Ammunition Column at AUTHIE (Square I 1.6) as soon as amount is known

A report will be rendered to this office of the amount handed over by each Battery.

4. Group Command will be handed over to 56th Divisional Artillery at 9 a.m. on 10th instant.

5. The G.O.C., R.A., 48th Division will be responsible for the Artillery support on the front covered by the 56th Division until 9 a.m. on the 11th May, 1916.

6. Acknowledge.

W.J.McLAY,
Major, R.A.,
Brigade Major,
56th Division.

Issued at   p.m.

Copy No.1 retained.

Copy No.2 to O.C. 1/2 London Brigade R.F.A.

Copy No.3 to O.C. 1/4 London (Howr.) Bde.,R.F.A.

Copy No.4 to Headquarters, 56th Division.

Copy No.5 to   do.   48th Division.

Copy No.6 to Headquarters, R.A., VII Corps.

SECRET   COPY NO 7

                              PLAN FOR R.A.

1.   The Artillery will be under the control of Lieut. Colonel
       MACDOWELL who will accompany Brigadier General NUGENT D.S.O.

2.   No Artillery will open fire without orders from Brigadier
       General NUGENT D. S. O.

3.   An officer of the 6' Howitzer Battery (1st Siege) will be with
       Lieut. Colonel MACDOWELL during the operations ready to bring
       on fire on the strong point K.11.c.6.5. if required.

4.   The Counter Battery work will be carried out by Batteries under
       arrangements made by Brigadier General NUGENT. D.S.O. An officer
       of the group will be with Lieut. Colonel MACDOWELL. Counter
       Batteries will open at once in the event of our Artillery
       opening a heavy fire.

5.   Two 4.5' Hows of the Divisional Artillery are to be used as
       Counter Batteries and will be attached to that group. The other
       two 4.5' Hows will be ready to engage enfilading trench K. 4.
       c. 9.5. to K. 4.d.1. 5.

6.   The group of four 18 pdr. Batteries will be ready to deal with
       machine gun emplacements in the front line trenches.

7.   Divisional Artillery of the 46th. & 48th. Divisions will
       co-operate as required. Detail may be given to Lieut.
       Col. MACDOWELL.

8.   Batteries not in action will stand by being in all ways ready
       to open fire at the shortest notice.
9.   Acknowledge.
                                      (SIGNED)   R.J.G.ELKINGTON.
                                            Brigadier General,
                                      Commanding 56th. Divisional Artillery

No. 1 copy retained.
No. 2   46th. Divisional Artillery.
No. 3   48th. Divisional Artillery.
No. 4   56th. Division.
No. 5   R. A. V11 Corps.
No. 6   167th. Infantry Brigade.
No. 7   O.C. 281st. Brigade R F A (56th. Div. Art. Group.)
No. 8   G.O.C. V11 Corps Heavy Artillery.

SECRET.   B.M. 433.

O.C. L.R.B.
      Kensingtons.
      Bde. M.G. Coy.
      281st. Bde, R.F.A.

H.Q. 56th. Division.
      167th. Infantry Brigade.

      With reference to operations for advancement of trench lines
on 56th. Divisional front.

      Work will be carried out by 167th. Bde. as follows -:
         1st. night   25th/26th.   Pegging.
         2nd. night   26th/27th.   Digging & wiring.
         3rd. night.   27th/28th.   Digging & wiring.

     Before daylight on the 25th. the L.R.B. establish a
post in the "Z" hedge which will be maintained until relieved by
covering troops of 167th Bde. on night 26th/27th. Special orders
have been issued to L.R.B. concerning this. (B.M.408 and B.M.423)

      W & Y Sectors having been subdivided into A.B.C.& D sub
sectors as already explained, Battalions of the 167th. Bde. have been
detailed to work as follows :-
        Subsector "A"   1st. Londons.
             "B"   8th. Middlesex.
             "C"   3rd. Londons.
             "D"   7th. Middlesex.

Machine Guns.   169th. Bde. M.G. Coy. has arranged for covering fire
if required from in or near the existing front line. On the 2nd & 3rd.
nights it will come temporarily under the command of B.G.C. 167th.
Brigade. Two guns have been allotted to each sub-sector. The officer
commanding each section of guns will be attached to the O.C. Battn.
of 167th. Brigade, of the sub-sector he is covering. The responsibility
of ordering fire to be opened rests with the B.G.C. 167th. Brigade,
who has arranged for telephonic communication accordingly. The machine
guns will remain in their covering positions and not be advanced to
the new line until orders are received from the B.G.C. 169th. Bde.

     The B.G.C. 169th. Bde. will take command of the new system when
the 167th. Bde. troops are relieved on the night 27th/28th.

     Covering troops for night 26th/27th. will be found from 167th.
Bde. except as notified to L.R.B. in B.M.423. Before the covering
troops withdraw on the 27th. posts of 1 officer, 1 N.C.O. and 10 men
with a Lewis gun and its personnel will be established in the new
line, as follows :-

Subsector "A"   Two posts to cover the BUCQUOY & PUISIEUX roads.
Subsector "B"   ONe post on the spur between the BUCQUOY road and the
               Chalk Cairn.
Subsector "C"   One post on the spur between the Chalk Cairn and the
               E corner of "Z" hegde.
Subsector D.   Two posts , One post in the N.E. corner of the "Z"
               hedge. One post at the point where Sap No.4 when
               continued will run into the bank in continuation
               of the "Z" hedge.

   During the 27th. these posts will deepen and strenghten their
positions as much as possible.

L.R.B. and Kensingtons have established ramps at places specified in B.M.399, and on the nights of the 26th/27th. and 27th/28th. will provide two men at each ramp to assist troops of the 167th. Bde, as much as possible.

L.R.B. and Kensingtons will ensure that on nights 26th/27th. and 27th/28th. the entire use of the communication trenches in their respective sectors is kept free for troops of 167th. Bde. between the hours of 8p.m. to 10p.m. and 1-30a.m. to 3 a.m. Special police will be detailed by them for this purpose.

No "VERY" lights or firing will take place from the present front line(except from W/47 & W/48 which will not be affected by above operations) during nights 26th/27th and 27th/28th.

(Signed) L.A.NEWNHAM, Capt.
Brigade Major,
169th. Infantry Brigade.

25th. May , 1916.

SECRET.

The Officer Commanding
    Heavy Artillery Group.

----

1. With reference to Secret 'Plan for R.A.' No.8 batteries as mentioned below will each have two guns laid on the undermentioned hostile batteries and will be ready to fire at a minute's notice on receipt of an order from Brigadier General NUGENT D.S.O. Headquarters, HEBUTERNE.

   "A" Zone   1/1 Kent H.B. R.G.A.   2 Guns   E.24.d.53.00.
   48th.H.A.G. ------------------   2 Guns   F.20.c.22.27.

   "B" Zone   283rd.A Battery R.F.A.   2 Guns   L.14.b.25.78.
   39th.H.A.G. 74th. S.Battery R.G.A.   2 Guns   L.I.a.44.15.
              114th. S. Battery R.G.A.   2 Guns   L.8.a.55.60.
              114th. S. Battery R.G.A.   2 Guns   L.8.d.20.40.

   "C" ZONE.   48th. H. Battery R.G.A.   (L.19b.12.48.
   17th. H.A.G. 11th. H.Battery R.G.A.   (L.26.d.85.85.
                                        (L.15.a.25.78.
                                        (I.20.d.33.37.

2. 73rd. Siege Battery R.G.A. will be ready to turn on fire on the strong point K.11.c5.8. if required, and for this purpose two Howitzers of this Battery will be laid on this point.
   Note. Strong point. K.11.c.5.8. to K.11.c.8.5.

3. Lieut. and Adjutant DAVSON will be with Brigadier General NUGENT, D.S.O. at his Headquarters at HEBUTERNE and also an officer of 73rd. S. Battery R.G.A. : O.C. 39th. H.A. Group will lay a direct line to these headquarters and also O.C. 73rd. S. Battery, R.G.A.

4. The method of communication to 48th. and 17th. H.A.Group will be from Headquarters, HEBUTERNE through 39th. H.A.Group.

Copies to :- Headquarters   56th. Division, R.A.
                                  Vlll Corps H.A.
                                  17th. H.A. Group.
                                  39th. H.A.Group.
                                  48th. H.A.Group.
                                  73rd. Siege Battery R.G.A.

Officer Commanding,
    281st. Brigade, R.F.A.

                      For your information.
                      Please acknowledge.

23-5-16.   (Signed) W.J.McLAY.
                                                           Major,
                                   Brigade Major R.A. 56th. Div.

Secret.   Copy No. 1

Reference Maps 1/10,000 57* D. N.E. 1,2,3,4.

                    Operation Order No. 1.D. 42
         By Lt. Col. C. C. MACDOWELL, commanding 56th. Div. Artillery Group.

INFORMATION.   (1) Divisional Operations will be carried out on four
                    successive days, under the command of Brig. Gen.
                    NUGENT. Dates to be notified later.

                (2) The Artillery will be under the control of Lt.
                    Colonel C. C. MACDOWELL.

ARTILLERY   The primary intentions of Artillery throughout the
                    operations will be –

INTENTION   (3) (a) To engage those special targets in enemy lines
                        which are worrying our infantry ; while preparing
                        or digging a fire trench in "NO MAN'S LAND".
                    (b) By establishing a protective barrage on
                        enemy's front line trenches, so as to enable
                        our working party to retire, and if necessary
                        bringing into action the 46th. and 49th. Div.
                        Artillery on the Northern and Southern flanks
                        respectively, and the counter Battery and Heavy
                        groups to deal with the enemy's Artillery.
                    (c) The last thing desired, however, is the
                        precipitation of a general Artillery engagement.
                    (d) Under no circumstances whatever will Battery
                        Commanders order GENERAL BARRAGE without distinct
                        order being given by Group Commander.

TARGETS.   (4) Targets which are allotted to 56th. Div.
                    Artillery Group Batteries will be within their
                    respective Trench Barrage Zones, as far as possible
                    with the exception of one section of "A" Battery
                    held in readiness to deal with special targets,
                    wherever required. One section of Howitzer Battery
                    will be allotted to commander Battery Group.
                                            Counter

                (5) The 46th and 49th. Div. Artillery will deal with
                    special objectives on the Northern and Southern
                    flanks of the Group Zones respectively and in
                    addition one section of the 46th. Div. Artillery
                    will take the place of the section of "A" Battery,
                    281st. Brigade, otherwise employed as above.

ORDERS.   (6) Operation orders will be issued to all concerned
                    for each night and day, during the operations.

COMMUNICATIONS. (7) The O. C. Artillery Group, who will accompany
                    Brig. Gen. NUGENT, will be in telephonic commu-
                    nication with Artillery, as shown on attached sheet
                    marked "Z".

Copy No 1 Ret. (8) Acknowledge.
    2 57th. Div. Art.   56th. Div. Artillery Group
    3 Counter Battery Group.
    4 Heavy Battery Group.
    5 46th. Div. Art.
    6 49th. Div. Art.
    7/11 Batteries, 56th. Div. Artillery Group.
    12 967th. Infantry Brigade.

SECRET.

Copy No. (1) ID 43.

Special Operations by the 56th. Division to be held on a
date to be notified later.

46th. Divisional Artillery.   39

(1) "Gunfire B"   With further reference to our I.D. dated
                   21/5/16 We have reduced your Zone considerably;
                   on receipt of word "Gunfire B" all guns and
                   howitzers will open fire at one round per gun per
    Rate of Fire   minute

                                Detail list of targets below –

                   No 1 Section – Enfilade K 4 C 25.88 to K4C 90.40.
                   No 2 Section – Enfilade K 4 A 15.55 to K4C 92.50
                   No 3 Section – Enfilade K 4 D 90.70 to K11A55.55
                                  support trenches.
                   No.4 Section – Enfilade K 5 C 02 to K 11B 13.32

                   Howitzers.   Code Word.

                   1 Gun   K 4 D   40. 74   " HOW EMMA "
                   1 Gun   K 5 C   10. 96   " HOW N "
                   1 Gun   K 4 D   24.73   " HOW O "
                   1 Gun   K 4 B   92.19   " HOW PIP."

(2) Howitzer Fire It may be desired to open fire with a single
        only   Howitzer gun on one of the above targets. In
                   this case the code word above will be passed over
                   the phone with the number of rounds required and
                   the rate of fire will be one round per gun per
    Rate of Fire. 30 seconds.

(3) Trench Barrage. In addition to the above one section of the
                   Lincoln Battery at J 12 d 5.6. may be required
                   to assist our Battery alongside it on front
                   Trench Barrage. If you have no objection
                   my Battery Commander will arrange this with
                   your Battery Commander direct.

(4)   The above arrangement will hold good
                   throughout the whole operations.

(5)   Details above amplify CRA 56th. Div. Secret
                   Letter. "PLAN for R.A." numbered S/CRA/205
                   dated 21/5/16.

(6)   Acknowledge.

SECRET   Copy No. I.D.44

Special Operations by the 48th. Division to be held

on a date to be notified later.

48th. Divisional Artillery.

(1)   With further reference to our I.D. 40 dated 11/5/16 no variation of the targets laid down for Field Guns and Howitzers has been made but please add the following code words to designate each Howitzer Target.

	Howitzers	Code Word.
	1 gun on strong point at K 11 C 8.7.	"How SS"
ANOTHER	1 gun on strong point at K 11 C 8.7.	"HOW SS TWO GUNS"

The Hows on the above strong points will search and sweep as may be necessary to deal with it.

1 GUN SEARCHING UP "SUNKEN ROAD" FROM K 17 a 7.8. K 11 d 3.0   "How Vic"   1 gun Searching up the "SUNKEN ROAD" from K 11 D 5.0. to K 11 D 8.1. "HOW VIC."

The rate of fire will be one round per gun per minute.

(2) SUNKEN SHOT.   On receipt of the code words "SUNKEN SHOT" the targets will be engaged.

(3) Howitzers Fire only   It may be desired to open fire with a single Howitzer gun on one of the above targets. In this case the code word above will be passed and the rate of fire will be as above mentioned.

(4)   The above arrangements will hold good throughout the whole Operations.

(5)   The details above amplify CRA 48th. Div. Secret Letter "PLAN for R.A." numbered S/CRA/295 dated 21/5/16.

(6)   Acknowledge.

Secret.   Copy No.

OPERATION ORDER No. I.D. 48.
By Lt. Col. C.C. MACDOWELL, commanding 48th. Div. Art. Group.

Night 26th/27th.

2nd. NIGHT.

(1) The 137th. Infantry Brigade will commence to dig
the new trench. The tapping and covering parties
will leave the communication trenches at 9-0p.m.
At 1-30a.m. the withdrawal of the working
parties will commence and at 2-0a.m. the covering
parties will withdraw, leaving posts in the line
for the day.

INFORMATION.

REPORT CENTRE.

(2) Brig. Gen. HUSSEY will be at the Report Centre at
O.P.H. and will be accompanied by Lt. Col. C.C.
MACDOWELL + an officer of the Counter Battery
Group and an officer from VII Corps, Heavy
Artillery. Lt. Col. WAINWRIGHT will be at 48th.
Div. Artillery Group Hd. Qrs. at V.L.B.

ARTILLERY. INTENTION.

(3) The intention of the Artillery will be as set
forth in my I.D. 42 dated 24-5-16, with the
following additional details.
The information, which will enable the Artillery
Commander to direct the fire of Batteries, will be
obtained —
  (a) from direct observation at O.P.H.
  (b) from 5 Artillery observers of 48th. Div.
      Art. Group, direct to O.P.H. via S.L.A.
  (c) from information received from Infantry
      by telephone and runner.

(4) In order to break the stillness of the night and
to detract the enemy's attention from the noise,
if any, of the digging, empty carts will be driven
up and down the SAILLY-BRAUTERNE road during the
night and a "4's" Howitzer of the 48th. Div. Art.
Group will fire enfilade at irregular intervals
over the length of the enemy's front line and drop
the shell in or about the TURKEY ROAD.

(5) In the event of the enemy discovering the party at
work and putting up either a centre or trench
Barrage the whole of our Artillery will reply,
but only on receipt of the order to do so from
O.P.H. with one exception below.
This will either silence the enemy sufficiently
to allow our infantry to continue to dig or cover
their retirement.
The exception referred to above is as follows —
In the event of the Artillery Officer at S.L.B.
not being able to establish communication with
O.P.H. by telephone by any of the routes indicated
on sheet marked "?" owing to the mine made by the
enemy's Artillery, he will decide whether to pass
the Code Words to the Field Artillery Groups and
the word to the Counter Battery and Heavy Groups
for a general engagement.
It must be clearly understood that under all
other circumstances the executive order to fire
must emanate from O.P.H.

TELEPHONE COMMUNICATIONS.

(6) The following orders must be strictly complied
with to ensure the best possible communication.
(a) No messages whatever, except those bearing on
the operations, will be passed over the telephone
between 9-0 p.m. and 4-0a.m.
(b) An officer must be continually

Secret.   Copy No.

TELEPHONE COMMUNICATIONS (contd.)

  (b) An officer must be continually at the telephone in every exchange, Battery and O.P.
  (c) All messages from O.P.O. will have priority over others.
  (d) Reports from O.P's will be sent via DLA and DPO (Monitor O.P. line)
  (e) All orders to fire will be prefixed with the words "OPEN MIRROR" and the operator or officer receiving the message will repeat it back.
  (f) Speech will be cut down to a minimum ; an example is attached.
  (g) Lines will be tested from O.P.O. and DLA backwards every quarter of an hour.
  (h) Linesmen will be held in readiness and sent out immediately on any line being reported out of order.
  (j) In the event of speech being impracticable owing to the noise of Artillery fire, buzzing will be resorted to , before giving up all idea of communication by telephone.
  (k) The above instructions and the code words to expect should be again fully explained to all telephonists and a list of code words and messages hung up in every telephonist's office.

RUNNERS. (1) If this proves useless , the linesmen will devolve into runners.

STAND TO. (2) All officers will be at their posts and all detachments on their guns throughout the night.

FOLLOWING
DAY 27th. (3) Half detachments will remain on the gun from 4 A.M. onwards and all Batteries must remain ready for immediate action all day.
    56th. Div. Art. O.P.'s will be continuously manned and on the bombardment of any of the occupied points of the new trench by the enemy O.P. officers will call for instant retaliation from battery concerned on enemy's front line and report immediately to Report Centre.

  (4) Acknowledge.

           56th. Div. Artillery Group

Issued at
26-5-1916.
 Copy 1 and 2 retained.
  3 56th. Div. Art.
  4 Corps, Heavy Group.
  5 46th. Div. Art. Group.
  6 49th. " " "
  7 Counter Battery Group.
  8/12 Batteries, 56th. Div. Art. Group.
  13 167th. Infantry Brigade.
  14 168th. Infantry Brigade.

Secret   Copy N° 1

Operation Order N° I.D. 49.
by Lt Col. C.C. Macdowell commdg. 56' Div. Arty. Group

           NIGHT 27¹/28¹

3ʳᵈ NIGHT	The 167ᵗʰ Infantry Brigade will continue the digging and strengthening of the new trench.
INFORMATION	The working hours will be as for the previous night.
ARTILLERY INTENTION	The instructions for the Artillery will be identical with those issued in my I.D. 48 for previous night. Reference para (4) of the above mentioned orders however, the 4.5 HOWITZER of 46' Div. Arty Group will not be required to specially fire as mentioned therein.
	The importance of all ranks being alert cannot be too strongly emphasised.
FOLLOWING DAY 28ᵗʰ	Half detachments will remain on the guns from 3.30 A.M. till receipt of further orders.

Issued at
27. 5. 16
Copy N° 1 & 2 retained
   3 56' Div Arty
   4 VII Corps H.A.
   5 39' H.A. Group
   6 46ᵗʰ Div. Arty.
   7 48ᵗʰ Div. Arty. Group
 8 to 12 Batteries 56' Div Arty Group
 13 - 167 Infantry Brigade
 14 - 169 Infantry Brigade

R.A. Lieut. for Adjt.
56' Div Arty Group.

Secret   Copy No 1

                    Orders No I D 46
By Lt Col. C.C. MacDowell commanding 56th Div Arty Group

1st Night   The Special Operation referred to in 56th D.O.
25th/26th   dated 24.5.16 will commence tonight at 9 P.M.
                    9 P.M. when our Infantry parties will go out to
                    peg and string the line.

INFORMATION
ARTILLERY   All Batteries of 56th Div Artillery Group will
                    stand to from 10 P.M. till dawn.

INTENTION   Telephonists should be alert in Batteries &
                    all other Groups.

NIGHT F.O.Os   56th Div Artillery Group will find 3 Night F.O.Os
                    to observe flashes and the condition of the front
                    during the night.

NIGHT LINES   The NIGHT LINES of 56th Div Artillery Group will be
                    on the "TRENCH BARRAGE". Barrage fire will not be
                    opened without orders from Group Headquarters.

RATE of FIRE   Rate of fire - 1 Round per gun per minute.
                    Batteries must be all ready prepared to deal as
                    ordered on receipt of orders with any Trench Mortars
                    Mortar etc and all parts of the TRENCH BARRAGE
                    which they can deal with in their zone.

REPORT CENTRE   REPORT CENTRE will be at 56th Div Artillery Group
                    Headquarters at SAILLY (F.L 13)

1st Day   56th Div Artillery Group's daily detachments will
                    be on guns during the day.

25.5.16   Orders as before
Issued at H.Q. 2.45 P.M.
Copy No 1 + 2 retained
          3 56 Div Arty
          4 3rd H.A. Group
          5 16th Div A.G.
          6 A.A. Battery
          7-11 Batteries 56th Div Arty Group
          12 167th Infantry Brigade

To O.C. 1/1st London Regt.
    1/3rd London Regt.
    1/7th Middlesex Regt.
    1/8th Middlesex Regt.
    2/1st Field Co.R.E.
    "B" Co. 5th Cheshire Regt.
    281st Bde.R.F.A.

G.418.
28-5-16.

The G.O.C.56th Division has received the following wire from Lieut.General Sir T.D.O'SNOW, K.C.B., Commanding VII Corps.

"The Corps Commander congratulates your Brigadier General NUGENT and all ranks of the 167th Brigade on the boldly conceived and gallantly executed work of the last two nights. It shows what can be done by troops who refuse to take the enemy at his own valuation. Both the Army Commander and the Commander-in-Chief yesterday expressed their satisfaction with the operation."

In forwarding the above message, the Brigadier General Commanding wishes to thank all ranks for the splendid way in which they have carried out an arduous and difficult task.

28-5-16.

Geo. Stewart, Captain,
Brigade Major,
167th. Inf.Bde.

107th. Infantry Bde.
26-5-16.

D

Dear Macdowell,

Thank you very much for the splendid way in which you and your fellows supported us last night and the night before.

It was of the greatest possible benefit to me to feel such absolute confidence in my Artillery Commander.

(signed)   FRANK NUGENT.

From Brigadier General NUGENT, D.S.O., Commanding 107th.
                Infantry Brigade.
To Lt. Col. C.C. MACDOWELL, Commanding 251st. Brigade, R.F.A.
            (36th. Div. Artillery Group.)

281st Brigade R.F.A.

War Diary

Month of June, 1916

WAR DIARY *or* **INTELLIGENCE SUMMARY**

Army Form C. 2118

March 1916 — 281 Brigade RFA / 1/2 London Brigade RFA

Place	Date	Hour	Summary of Events and Information	Remarks and references to Appendices
SAILLY	1st		A notable though gradually increasing activity is taken place on the front. The enemy during registration of new battery positions & hostile manoeuvre heavy action at night. Our batteries by co-operating & by imaginary general fire have a close watch & great work some sites	
	5th		Battery Sgt. Major's name appears in Birthday Honours Gazette	
	7th		1st & 3rd sections of our Coast and Lique North Zillebeke appear ready for shift of our front. Meanwhile A+B batteries batter positions are being dug and advanced positions commenced to dig near advanced position Kanonweg & from in old positions at the same time work very arduous & trying. All ranks working cheerfully.

WAR DIARY or INTELLIGENCE SUMMARY

Army Form C. 2118

281 Brigade RFA late 1/2 LONDON BRIGADE

Month: June

Place	Date	Hour	Summary of Events and Information	Remarks and references to Appendices
SAILLY	15th		The following Officers and NCOs "Mentioned in Despatches" of this day. Lt-Col C.C. MACDOWELL, MAJOR ODAM, CAPT & ADJUTANT. R.T. LEE No 1234. BSM. MARRIOTT and No 045 Bdr HOGBEN all for services at LOOS. Brigade Major have moved up to HENU	
	16		A + B now ordered out of action & guns taken over by Northern Group. The Jordan Group area now divided into two, the Southern Group covering that area from NAMELESS FARM 1000 yards S of GOMMECOURT to SUNKEN ROAD HEBUTERNE - PUISIEUX road. Southern Group consists of A, B, C, D (How) batteries 281 Brigade + 109 Battery RFA under OC 281 Brigade	

JUNE 1916 281 Bde all RFA

WAR DIARY or INTELLIGENCE SUMMARY
Army Form C. 2118

Place	Date	Hour	Summary of Events and Information	Remarks and references to Appendices
SAILLY	21		A B & 109 Batteries came into action, in what positions unclear	Appendix A
	22		Actual in left at the trench were marked	
	24	(U day) Commenced general bombardment all batteries in action throughout the night. Fire very steady. A/281 1050 rounds fired. B Battery slightly hit by gas shells no casualties. D Battery 109 (today) 2 men wounded. 1 man wounded C/C. 1 man wounded (gas). 1 man killed. Numbers of rounds	
	25	(V day) Active operations continued total number of rounds fired 1602	

WAR DIARY or INTELLIGENCE SUMMARY

Army Form C.2118

281 Brigade RFA

Month: June 1916

Place	Date	Hour	Summary of Events and Information	Remarks and references to Appendices
SAILLY	26th	(W. day)	active operations continued, number of rounds fired 5530.	
"	27th	(X. day)	artillery bombardment continued, number of rounds fired 7056	
"	28th	(Y. day)	artillery bombardment continued, number of rounds fired 8893.	
	29th	(Y1. day)	attack by infantry postponed for 48 hours, artillery bombardment continued, number of rounds fired 5300	
	30th	(Y2. day)	artillery bombardment continued, number of rounds fired 5300.	

(signed)
LIEUT. COLONEL
COMMANDING 281 BRIGADE,
ROYAL FIELD ARTILLERY.

SECRET.   Copy No.

REF. MAPS. (1/10000 57 D. N.E. 1.2.3. 4.   Edn. 2. B.
           (1/5000 GOMMECOURT.

Operation Orders No.I.DB 80. by Lt. Col. C.C. MACDOWELL, commanding
                        Southern Artillery Group.

COMPOSITION OF GROUP.
(1)   The Southern Group will consist of four 18 pdr.Batteries
-: 109th. Battery, R.F.A. 281/A. 281/B. 281/C and 1
HOW Battery 281/D, affiliated at Zero to the 108th.
Infantry Brigade.

GROUP FRONT LINE SYSTEM.
(2)   During the operations until "Z" day at Zero the phrase
"FRONT LINE SYSTEM" means for the Southern Group :-
      Junction FEVER-EPTE along the front line trenches
to junction FAIR-ARUN ; up ARUN to junction FAN, thence
FABLE. FAIN. FELON, back to junction with EPTE, down
EPTE to junction EPTE-FEVER. All trenches inside this
system , also communication trenches EPTE. ELDE. ANNA.
ANT. ARUN. to the second line system.

BATTERY FRONT LINE SYSTEM.
(3)   The Group Front Line SYSTem is divided by Batteries as
      follows :-
          109th. Batt. - FETTER. FELT. FELON. EPTE. ELDE. ET.
          "A"   "   - FALL. FAIR. FABLE. FACE. FATE.
          "B"   "   - FARMER. FARMYARD. FARM.
          "C"   "   - FAIR. FANCY. FAN. FAST.
          "D" HOW. "   - The whole of the GROUP FRONT LINE
                        SYSTEM.

(4)   Every officer in each Battery must know the exact
      programme for his Battery , especially on "Z" day
      - so that if communications break the Battery can still
      carry on according to Time Table until communication
      can be re-established.

(5)   The importance of keeping these orders absolutely
      SECRET amongst Officers until "Z" day is to be clearly
      explained to all concerned.
          On "Z" day a written copy of Time Table should be
      in possession of each No. 1.

(6)   From 4-0 P.M. to 4-30 P.M.daily , except on "Z" day
      all fire will cease to enable photos to be taken.

(7)   Enemy O.P.'s mentioned in Operation Orders will be dealt
      with throughout "Y" "X" & "Z" days by the
      Batteries concerned.

(8)   Acknowledge.

                                    _____
                                    Commanding Southern Artillery
                                               Group.

Copy No. 1 & 2 retained.
         3 - 56th. Div. Artillery.
         4 - 108th. Infantry Brigade.
         5 - 9 Batteries of the Group.
         10 - Northern Artillery Group.

HOURS.

RELIEFS.
(1) Battery Commanders should, as far as possible, organise definite reliefs on the guns.

O.P. OFFICERS.
(2) The O.C. A&B. Battery will detail an officer for duty from dawn to dusk at O.P.1.

The O.C.'s C & D Batteries will each detail an officer for duty from dawn to dusk at O.P.2.

The O.C.'s A & B Batteries will each detail an officer for duty from dawn to dusk at Central O.P.

An officer's tour of duty should be 4 hours - times of relief should be at the hours of 4- a.m.   12 noon.   8- p.m.

LIAISON
OFFICERS.
Officers Commanding Right Batteries will detail an officer for duty at Infantry Brigade H.Q. until such ... Day ..., "A" Batteries one evening, "B" Battery on the day, "C" Battery on and on.
Tour of duty from 8-0 P.M. to dawn.

KEEPING
WIRE CUT.
(4) In keeping wire open in front of their battery front line system, on night following "T" all Batteries will fire on wire from North to South and South to North in series alternately.
Lanes which have been cut by machine gun Group during the day will be notified to Battery Commanders by 9-0 P.M.
These lanes should receive 50% of the ammunition allotted for firing on wire.
If no lane has been cut in Battery's zone fire will be evenly distributed over the whole wire in that zone.

SALVOS.
(5) Salvoes will be fired, as far as possible, both by day and night at irregular intervals.

DISTRIBUTION
OF FIRE.
Batteries, as a rule will be active at the following times :-
A Battery - hour to 20 minutes after.
(6) B " - 15 minutes past to 35 minutes past the hour.
C " - 30 minutes past to 50 minutes past the hour.
D " - commencing at 10 minutes past & ... 40 minutes past the hour.
... - 45 minutes past to 5 minutes past the hour.

During the general bombardment by day O.C.'s will arrange that rounds allotted to trenches in the nature however of short bursts of fire, at irregular intervals, when the battery is active.

OBSERVATION
OF FIRE.
All fire must be carefully ... whenever possible to do so.
(7)

SECRET.   I.D. 22

                              "U" DAY.
Batt.   Time.   Operations.   AMN.

"A"   During   (a) Normal Registration.   as required.
       DAY.

       NIGHT.   (1) Salvoes front line wire. FATE.   50 rds. S.

                  (2) Salvoes on road - point 16
                      through point 03 to trench
                      MAIN and from path 04 to 03.   200 rds. S.

"B"   During   (a) Normal Registration.   as required.
       DAY.

       NIGHT.   (1) Salvoes on wire in front line
                      and wire FARMER.   50 rds. S.
                  (2) Salvoes on tracks from 03 to
                      N.W. edge of ROSSIGNOL WOOD (1 section)
                      and tracks N. of ANNA and S. of ANT (1 section)
                      and these trenches.   200 rds. S.

"C"   During   (a) Normal Registration.   as required.
       DAY.

       NIGHT.   (1) Salvoes front line wire
                      FAIR. FACE.   50 rds. S.
                  (2) Salvoes on trench ARUN : track
                      by ARUN and track from STRONG
                      POINT to ARUN.   200 rds. S.

"D"   During   (a) Normal Registration.   as required.
       DAY.
HOWS.
       NIGHT.   (1) Normal Retaliation.   as required.

169th. During   (a) Normal Registration.   as required.
       DAY.

       NIGHT.   (1) Salvoes front line wire FETTER.   50 rds. S.
                 (2) Salvoes on trenches ELBE, ET.
                     and EPTE up to MESS & MERE.   200 rds. S.

SECRET.   "V" DAY.   I.D.

Batt.	Time.		Operations.	AMM.
"A"	During DAY.	(a)	Bombardment of front system of trenches and communication trenches - FATE. FAME. FABLE. FALL. FACT.	500 H.E.
	12-0 noon to 12-30 p.m.	(b)	Bombardment of O.P.'s and second line trenches to allow MORTARS to register unseen.	100 S. 125 H.E.
	NIGHT.	(1) (2)	Keeping open wire as on "U" night. Roads and tracks as on "U" night.	350 S.
"B"	During DAY.	(a)	Bombardment of front system of trenches and communication trenches - FARMYARD. FARMER. FARM	500 H.E.
	12-0 noon to 12-30 p.m.	(b)	Same as for "A" Battery	(125 H.E. (100 S.
	NIGHT.	(1) (2)	Same as for "U" night. Same as for "U" night.	350 S.
"C"	During DAY.	(a)	Bombardment of front system of trenches and communication trenches - FAIR. FACE. FANCY. FAT. FAN. FAST. ARUN.	500 H.E.
	12-0 noon to 12-30 p.m.	(b)	Same as for "A" Battery.	(125 H.E. (100 S.
	NIGHT.	(1) (2)	Same as for "U" night. Same as for "U" night.	350 S.
"D"	During DAY.	(a)	Trench junctions and selected points namely - Points 94. 16. 98. 84. 38. 61. 33 Junctions - FAN-FABLE. FANCY-FACT. ET-FALL. ELBE-FELT and "NAMELESS FARM".	250 302 H.E.
	7-15 p.m.	(b)	Bombardment of BUCQUOY. Appendix D.V.	48 H.E.
	NIGHT.	(1)	Salvoes on Roads and tracks - points to be notified from Group.	--Ammunition as reqd.
109th.	During DAY.	(a)	Bombardment of front system of trenches and communication trenches - FETTER. FELT. FELON. EPTE. ELBE. ET.' - special attention to EPTE.	500 H.E.
	12 noon to 12-30 p.m.	(b)	Same as for "A" Battery.	(125 H.E. (100 S.
	NIGHT.	(1) (2)	Same as for "U" night. Same as for "U" night.	350 S.

SECRET   I.D.

"W" DAY.

Batt.	Time.		Operations.	AMM.
"A"	During DAY.	(a)	Bombardment of front line trench system.	390 H.E
	9-45a.m. to 10-25 a.m.	(b)	Intense Bombardment in conjunction with Heavy Artillery & smoke : increasing bombardment in intensity during last 15 minutes.	225 H.E 190 S.
	10-25 a.m.	(c)	Lift for 5 minutes on trenches near S.W. edge of ROSSIGNOL WOOD.	
	10-30 a.m.	(d)	Back to front line system.	
	NIGHT.	(1)	Salvoes on tracks and roads as laid down for "U" night.	475 S.
"B"	During DAY.	(a)	Bombardment of front line trench system.	390 H.E.
	9-45 a.m. to 10-25a.m.	(b)	Same as for "A" Battery.	225 H.E. 190 S.
	10-25 a.m.	(c)	Lift for 5 minutes on to MEET and N.W. edge of ROSSIGNOL WOOD.	
	10-30 a.m.	(d)	Back to front line system.	
	NIGHT.	(1)	Same as for "U" night.	575 S.
"C"	During DAY.	(a)	Bombardment of front line trench system.	390 H.E 225 H.E.
	9-45 a.m. to 10-25a.m.	(b)	Same as for "A" Battery	190 S.
	10-25 a.m.	(c)	Lift for 5 minutes on to MALT. *Mat Map & Main*	
	10-30 a.m.	(d)	Back to front line system.	
	NIGHT.	(1)	Same as for "U" night.	475 S.
"D" HOW.	During DAY.	(a)	Bombardment of special points in front line system. All cross junctions of communication trench EPTE (2) ELBE(3) ET (2) POINTS 98. 03. and cross intersections of ARUN (5)	75 100 H.E
	9-45a.m. to 10-25a.m.	(b)	Same as for "A" Battery (trench junctions)	
	10-25a.m.	(c)	Lift for 5 minutes on to trench junctions N.W. of MESS. MERE. MEED. MEET. After 10 rounds on each on to the 4 trench junctions, S.W. edge ROSSIGNOL WOOD.	225 300 H.E.
	10-30a.m.	(d)	Back to front line trench system.	
	NIGHT.	(1)	At points where communication trenches cross the road at 61. 16. 03 and K. 12 Central.	75 100 H.E
		(2)	In addition "D" Battery fire at intervals during the night on L.2.d.4.8. L.8.d.1.1. L.8.Central. L.8.a.9.6.	75 100 H.E
109th.	During DAY.	(a)	Bombardment of front line system. particularly EPTE.	390 H.E
	9-45a.m. to 10-25a.m.	(b)	Same as for "A" Battery.	225 H.E
	10-25a.m.	(c)	Lift for 5 minutes on to MESS. MERE. and MEED.	100 S.
	10-30a.m.		Back to front line system.	
	NIGHT.	(1)	Same as for "U" night.	475 S.

SECRET.   I.D.
                        "X" DAY.

Batt.	Time.		Operations.	AIM.
"A"	During DAY.	(a)	Bombardment of front line system as for "W" day.	635 H.E
	5-5 to 5-45a.m. 5-15 to 5-55 AM	(b)	Intense bombardment with smoke, increasing in intensity during the last 15 minutes.	100 H.E 50 S.
	6-25 to 7-5a.m. PM	(c)	Intense bombardment cooperating with smoke and heavy Artillery, increasing in intensity during the last 15 minutes.	335 H.E.
	7-5a.m. PM	(d)	Lift for 5 minutes as for "W" day.	175 S.
	NIGHT.	(1)	TRACKS, roads and selected points. Road from "HAPLESS FARM" through point 83 to ARUN junction. Road from point 84 to point 83.	400 S.
"B"	During DAY.	(a)	Same as for "A" Battery.	655 H.E
	5-5 to 5-45a.m. 5.15 to 5.55 AM	(b)	Same as for "A" Battery.	200 H.E. 100 S.
	6-25 to 7-5a.m. PM	(c)	Same as for "A" Battery.	335 H.E 175 S.
	7-5a.m. PM	(d)	Lift same as for "A" Battery.	
	NIGHT.	(1)	Road North of ANNA to ANT. Trenches ANNA and ANT. Road S. of ANT.	400 S.
"C"	During DAY. 5.15 to 5.55 AM	(a)	Same as for "A" Battery.	655 H.E
	5-5 to 5-45a.m.	(b)	Same as for "A" Battery.	100 H.E 50 S.
	6-25 a.m. to 7-5a.m. PM	(c)	Same as for "A" Battery	335 H.E 175 S.
	7-5a.m. PM	(d)	Lift same as for "A" Battery.	
	NIGHT.	(1)	Trench junctions in 3rd line (7 points) Trench junctions Trench NESS to MAIN (6 points) ARUN road to STRONG POINT and trench MAIN.	400 S.
"D" HOW.	DURING DAY. 5.15 to 5.55 AM	(a)	Same as for "W" day.	135 H.E 105
	5-5 to 5-45a.m.	(b)	Trench junctions at STRONG POINT - Intense bombardment accompanied by smoke.	70 155 H.E
	6-25 to 7-5a.m. PM	(c)	Trench junctions in 3rd. line system from FRESH to FAST (9 points)	140 325 H.E
	7-5a.m. PM	(d)	Lift for 5 minutes on to Trench junctions from NESS to MAIN. (10 points)	140 70
	NIGHT.	(1)	Trench junctions in 3rd line (7 points) Trench junctions from TRENCH NESS to MAIN (8 points)	70 155 H.E
109th.	During DAY. 5.15 to 5.55 AM	(a)	Same as for "A" Battery.	655 H.E
	5-5 to 5-45a.m.	(b)	Same as for "A" Battery.	100 H.E 50 S.
	6-25 to 7-5a.m. PM	(c)	Same as for "A" Battery with special attention to NPTE.	335 H.E 175 S.
	7-5a.m. PM NIGHT.	(d) (1)	Lift same as for "A" Battery. Trenches and NPTE. ANNE. NE.	400 S.

SECRET.   I.D.
                            "X" DAY.

Batt. Time.   Operations.   AMM.

"A"   During   (a) Bombardment of front line system
      DAY   and O.P.'s   645 H.E.
      6-45 to   (b) Intense bombardment with smoke
      7-25 a.m.   increasing in intensity during the   180 H.E.
                      last 15 minutes.   100 S.
      4-45 to   (c) Intense bombardment with heavy
      5-25 p.m.   Artillery and smoke increasing   500 H.E.
                      in intensity during the last 15 minutes.   500 S.
      5-25 p.m.   (d) Lift for 5 minutes on to S.W. edge of   250 H.E
                      ROSSIGNOL WOOD.   250 S
      5-30 p.m.   (e) Back to front line system.

      NIGHT.   (1) Salvoes on tracks and roads as for "X"
                      night.   600 S.

"B"   During   (a) Same as for "A" Battery.   645 H.E
      DAY.
      6-45 to   (b) Same as for "A" Battery.   180 H.E
      7-25 a.m.   100 S.
      4-45 to   (c) Same as for "A" Battery.
      5-25 p.m.   250   500 H.E
                                                             250   500 S.

      5-25 p.m.   (d) Lift for 5 minutes on to MEET.
      5-30 p.m.   (e) Back to front line system.

      NIGHT.   (1) Same as for "X" night.   700 S.

"C"   During   (a) Same as for "A" Battery.   645 H.E
      DAY.
      6-45 to   (b) Same as for "A" Battery.   180 H.E
      7-25 a.m.   100 S.
      4-45 to   (c) Same as for "A" Battery.   250   500 H.E
      5-25 p.m.   250   500 S.
      5-25 p.m.   (d) Lift for 5 minutes on to MALT. MAP.
                      MAT. MAIN.
      5-30 p.m.   Back to front line system.

      NIGHT.   (1) Same as for "X" night.   600 S.

"D"   During   (a) Same as for "A" Battery.   230 H.E
      DAY.
      6-45 to   (b) Intense bombardment on trench junctions
      7-25 a.m.   in front system.   65 H.E.
      8-15 a.m.   (c) 3 minutes bombardment of BUCQUOY   as in
                      Appendix D.Y.   48 H.E.
      4-45 to   (d) Intense bombardment of front line system
      5-25 p.m.   particularly trench junctions about
                      STRONG POINT.   230 H.E
      5-25 p.m.   (e) Lift on to trench junctions in second   115
                      system of trenches 5 minutes.
      5-30 p.m.   (f) Return to front line system.

      NIGHT.   (1) Salvoes on track and roads including
                      L.2.d.4.3. L.2.d.i.i. L.T. Central.   75
                      L.3.a. 0.3.   100 H.E

109th. During   (a) Same as for "A" Battery.   645 H.E
       DAY.
       6-45 to   (b) Same as for "A" Battery and bombardment   180 H.E
       7-25 a.m.   of STRONG POINT.   100 S.
       4-45 to   (c) Same as for "A" Battery.   100 H.E
       5-25 p.m.
       5-25 p.m. (d) Lift for 5 minutes on to MESS. MERE. MEED.
       5-30 p.m. (e) Back to front line system.   250 500 H.E
                                                                250 500 S.

       NIGHT.   (1) Same as for "X" night.   600 S.

SECRET.   I.D. 83.

Map References 1/20,000. 57D. N.E.
            APPENDICES D.V. & D.Y.   D/281 Battery only.

Bombardment of BUCQUOY.

    The following system will be adopted in the Bombardment of BUCQUOY on - "V" Day 7-15 P.M. & on "Y" day 8-15 A.M. On each day the amount of ammunition allowed is 48 rounds of H.E. and it will be distributed over the southern portion of the town.

    The fire will be in Salvoes at irregular intervals :-

    Open on CROSS ROADS, centre of town near Church, 8 rounds of H.E.

    Search up to point 1247 - 12 rounds of H.E.

    Search from point 1236 to point 139 - 12 rounds of HE.

    Bombardment of CROSS ROADS due W. of Y. of BUCQUOY - 16 rounds. H.E.

             [signature]
             Commanding Southern Artillery Group.

SECRET

Copy No. 6

OPERATION ORDER NO.4

by

BRIGADIER GENERAL R.JG.ELKINGTON, C.M.G.

COMMANDING 56th DIVISIONAL ARTILLERY.

20th June, 1916.

1. The object of the VIIth Corps attack in the forthcoming operations will be for the Corps to establish itself on a line which runs approximately on our present line about 250 yards North East of the 16 POPLARS - EAST of NAMELESS FARM - along the ridge in K.5.a. and E.29.c., to the Little "Z", and thence back to the British line.

2. The attack of the 56th Division will be carried out by the 168th Brigade and 169th Brigade whose tasks will be as follows :-

(a) The objectives of the 168th Brigade will be to capture the German Line from FAIR Trench about K.11.d.1.3 along FARM, FAME, ELBE, FELON, to a point in FELL 50 yards North West of the Trench junction at K.5.c.5.2, and to establish itself in three strong points :-

  1. About FARM YARD, FARMER and FARM.
  2. About Trench ELBE between ET and FELON.
  3. About cross Trenches of FELL and FELON with EPTE.

168th Brigade will be responsible for construction of a fire Trench facing South East to connect right flank of captured line to our present line in W.47.

(b) The task of the 169th Brigade will be carried out in three phases. The objectives of the 169th Brigade in the first phase will be to capture the line of German Trenches from the left of the 168th Brigade along FELL, FELLOW, FEUD, THE CEMETERY, ECK, THE MAZE, EEL, and FIR, and to establish three strong points :-

  1. From FEUD through EMS to the CEMETERY inclusive.
  2. About the MAZE.
  3. About the South East corner of GOMMECOURT PARK (i.e. the junction of FIR and FIRM trenches).

The second phase of 169th Brigade attack will take place immediately after the first phase.
The objective of the second phase is the quadrilateral of Trenches in the South East portion of K.5.a.
The Artillery lifts will be timed on the assumption that Infantry will reach EMS (between ETCH and FILLET) 25 minutes after Zero; and EXE (between ETCH and FILLET) 27 minutes after Zero time.
EXE Trench will be blocked about K.5.a.4.4 and communication established with FEUD and FELLOW, via EMS and ETCH respectively.

The Third phase will commence directly the quadrilateral is captured, and will consist in securing the cross Trenches at K.5.a.7.8. (Where INDUS crosses FILL and FILLET) and joining hands with 46th Division along FILL. FILLET will be consolidated facing East.
The Artillery lifts will be timed on the assumption that Infantry reach the Cross Trenches at K.5.a.7.8 by 35 minutes after Zero time.

56th DIVISIONAL ARTILLERY

The Divisional Artillery will be Grouped as follows :-

NORTHERN GROUP under Lieutenant Colonel SOUTHAM

3 Batteries 18 pdr until Zero on Z day, then 4 Batteries.
1 Battery 4.5" Howitzers.
Affiliated at Zero to the 169th Infantry Brigade.

SOUTHERN GROUP under Lieutenant Colonel MACDOWELL

4 Batteries 18 pdr.
1 Battery 4.5" Howitzers.
Affiliated at Zero to 168th Infantry Brigade.

WIRE CUTTING GROUP under Lieutenant Colonel PRECHTEL

5 Batteries 18 pdr. until Zero on Z day, then 4 Batteries.
1 Battery 4.5" Howitzers.

Two of the guns of this Howitzer Battery will be at the call of the Counter Battery Group.

A/280 Battery, Wire Cutting Group will come under the orders of the Officer Commanding NORTHERN GROUP at Zero on Z day. Officer Commanding NORTHERN GROUP will therefore issue beforehand to this Battery all Operation Orders that may be necessary as to the fire of this Battery after Zero hour.

Wire Cutting Group will be under the direct orders of the Divisional C.R.A. with the exception of the two guns for Counter Battery Group.

All night firing will be done by Group-Commanders in consultation with Infantry Brigadiers.

The programme is as per schedule attached.

The Officers Commanding NORTHERN and SOUTHERN Groups will each detail an officer to be attached to each of the battalions in the front line in their respective Groups on Z day. These officers will be accompanied by 1 N.C.O., two telephonists, and a telephone.

Arrangements have been made for an officer of the VIIth Corps Heavy Artillery Group to be with each Infantry Brigade on Z day.

Each R.A. Group is to have a specially selected observing Officer in direct communication with the Group Commander whose duties will be to send back all information which he can gather from the front of his Group on Z day.

Headquarters 56th Divisional Artillery will be at SOUASTRE on Z day; reports will constantly be sent in by Group Commanders.

NOTES

1. Times must be adhered to, not number of rounds, which latter are a guide and not the controlling factor.

2. From 4.0 pm. to 4.30 pm. daily except Z day all fire will cease to enable photos to be taken.

3. O.P's as per list will be dealt with by Howitzers and 18 pdrs throughout Y day.

4. The term "FRONT LINE SYSTEM" means

(a) <u>NORTHERN GROUP</u> Front Line Trench from K.4.c.1.7 to junction FEVER-EPTE, thence up EPTE to junction with FELL thence to junction FILM-EXE, then K.4.b.5.0 to K.4.b.4.2 to K.4.d.10.95 to K.4.a.95.30 to K.4.a.6.4 back to K.4.c.1.7 and all trenches inside this, also communication trenches EPTE, ETCH, EMS.

(b) <u>SOUTHERN GROUP</u> Junction FEVER-EPTE along front line to junction FAIR-ARUN up ARUN to junction with FAN thence FABLE-FAME -FELON to junction with EPTE down EPTE to junction with FEVER and all trenches inside this, also communication trenches ANNA-ANT-ELBE -EPTE.

4.   1172 exchanged,   400.
5.   —   400
6.   960 exchanged.   400
109   —   400 tomorrow

SECRET

3.　　The 167th Brigade, less the following detachments, will be in Divisional Reserve in HEBUTERNE. :-

　　167th Brigade Headquarters will be in SOUASTRE, but they will establish an advanced Headquarters in HEBUTERNE at K.15.b.2.9 (the present right Brigade Headquarters).

(a)　　1 Coy. 167th Brigade will be placed at the disposal of the Brigadier General Commanding 169th Brigade to hold Y 49 - Y 50.

(b)　　Seven officers and 200 other ranks of 167th Brigade will be detailed for the control of smoke, and will be under the orders of the Divisional Gas Officer, under arrangements already issued to all concerned.

(c)　　Approximately 1200 men will be required for work under the C.R.E. on communication trenches across "NO MANS LAND", and for carrying parties for R.E. Stores.

(d)　　The attack will be carried out under cover of smoke.

4.　　The preliminary bombardment will be carried out for a period of 5 days; and the attack will be made on the 6th day.

　　A programme of the preliminary bombardment is embodied in these orders.

　　During the days V, W, X, Y, there will be false smoke attacks which will be accompanied by an intense bombardment of the enemy's trenches, communications and batteries.

SECRET.   I.D. 90.

   AMENDMENTS.
   ----

(1)   The Infantry Battalions in line are making
Reconnaissances of German wire and trenches after
the wire-cutting has taken place each day, as follows :-
    U/V night.   11-0 p.m. to 12 midnight.
    V/W night.   1-0 a.m. to 2-0 a.m.
    W/X night.   12 midnight to 1-0 a.m.
    X/Y night.   11-0 p.m. to 12 midnight.
During these hours Batteries will only fire on Targets
in rear of the German front line system.

(2)   Under no circumstances will Battery Fire be
employed during the Operations, as it has been found
that Batteries have been more easily discovered when
this nature of Fire has been employed.

(3) INTENSE BOMBARDMENT.
         In connection with the phrase "INTENSE
BOMBARDMENT" the word "INTENSE" is intended to convey
that the maximum rate of fire should be maintained at
irregular intervals distributed over the times laid
down, in bursts, of as many rounds as allotment of
ammunition allows.

(4) TIME. BAROMETER. & THERMOMETER.
         Signal time will be passed to Units twice daily
at 10-0 a.m. and 6-0 p.m.
         Barometer & Thermometer readings twice daily
at 10-0 a.m. & 6-0 p.m.

(5) ALLOTMENT OF AMMUNITION.   "D/241" only.
    "U" DAY.   No Change.

    "V" DAY.   for During Day   (a) read 540 H.E.
                                 (b) "   40 H.E.
                Night.   (b) "   Ammunition
                                         as required.

    "W" DAY.   for During Day   (a) read 70 H.E.
                                 (b) "
                                 (c) "
                Night.   (a) "   70 H.E.
                                 (c) "   70 H.E.

    "X" DAY.   for During Day   (a) read 150 H.E.
                                 (b) "
                                 (c) "
                                 (d) "
                Night.   (a) "

    "Y" DAY.   for During Day   (a) read
                                 (b) "
                                 (c) "

                                 (d) "
                                 (e) "
                Night.   (f) "   70   "

    "Z" DAY.   for Summary DAY
                Before - 30 min (a) read 300 H.E.
                                (b) "   150 "
    ----
(6)   "Z" DAY before Zero Time.
    D. How's.   "   " (b)
    Howh.   "   " (b)

SECRET.   I.D. 91.

Second List of "AMENDMENTS."

Operation Orders No. I.D. 82 are hereby amended as follows,
(Authority - S/C.R.A./ 239/2.

(1)   "X" Day.
       Times for Intense Bombardment for :-
       5-5 to 5-45 A.M.   read   "5-15 to 5-55 A.M."
       6-25 to 7-5 A.M.   "   "6-25 to 7-5 P.M."
and for at "7-5 A.M. lift for 5 minutes" read at 7-5 P.M.
lift for 5 minutes.

(2)   "W. X. & Y."

       For "Bombardment to increase in intensity during
last 15 minutes" read "Bombardment to increase in
intensity during the last 10 minutes",

(3)   SMOKE DISCHARGE.
       Smoke discharge in co-operation with intense
Artillery Bombardment will take place as follows :-
       "W" DAY.   10-15 A.M. to 10-25 A.M.

       "X" DAY.   5-45 A.M. to 5-55 A.M.

       "Y" DAY.   7-15 A.M. to 7-25 A.M.

In addition to W. X. & Y. days SMOKE will be used on

"Z" Day only.

281st BRIGADE.
R.F.A.

SECRET.   I.D. ...

O.P.'s and Suspected O.P.'s

O.P.'s must be dealt with systematically and the attack should be sudden and severe for at least three minutes.

The fire must be most accurate and therefore O.P.'s should be registered beforehand and "H.E" only should be used - 4'5 Hows' and 18 pdrs. should co-operate and fire simultaneously.

After about 3 minutes 18 pdrs. should dust adjacent trenches with Shrapnel.

The located enemy's O.P.'s in the Southern Group are :-

> K. 11. a. 97. 72. (first system)
>
> Position at B.M. 130.5 in rear of
>
> "NAMELESS FARM".

Battery Commanders should arrange in dealing with these to co-operate, or when any other O.P.'s or suspected O.P.'s are discovered.

MINNENWERFER.

Hostile MINNENWERFER locations in Group Front Line System, and Batteries which should deal with them on the nights "U" "V" and "W" and subsequent nights, if necessary :-

K. 17. & 22. 72. (MINNY South) (S. of SUNKEN ROAD.)		"C" & "D"
K. 11. d. 95. 90. (MINNY ARUN) (Second line junction of trench ARUN)		"C" & "D"
K. 11. a. 90. 90. (MINNY FAME)		"B" & "D"
K. 11. d. 90. 90. (MINNY FABLE)		109th. & "D"

A couple of Salvoes in the early part of the night and at 1-30 a.m. has been found very useful in keeping these MORTARS quiet.

"D" Battery will deal with all of these when firing on trench junctions.

SECRET.   I.D. No. 102.

OPERATION ORDERS BY LT. COL. C. C. MACDOWELL, Commanding the MACART GROUP.

(1) To-morrow the 29th. inst., will be known as Y.1. DAY.

The 30th. inst., will be known as Y.2. DAY.

(2) Programme for the Group is attached.

(3) There will be a pause of 30 minutes each day to enable photographs to be taken. This pause will be :-

    Y.1.   3-0 p.m. to 3-30 p.m.

    Y.2.   3-30 p.m. to 4-0 p.m.

(4) Heavy Artillery Bombardments will take place each day - but these will be without the co-operation of the Divisional Artillery.

(5) There will be an intense Bombardment by the Divisional Artillery daily, time to be notified later.

June/28/16.

SECRET.   I.D. No. 122.

OPERATION ORDER (No. 6) by BRIGADIER GENERAL ELKINGTON. C. B. E.
        COMMANDING   56th.   DIVISIONAL ARTILLERY.
_____

                                                      28th. June/1916.
(1)
        To-morrow 29th.inst., will be known as Y.1. Day.
        The 30th. inst., will be known as Y.2. Day.

(2)   Programmes for various Groups and allotment of ammunition are
        attached.

(3)   There will be a pause of 30 minutes each day to enable
        photographs to be taken.
                This pause will be :-
                    Y.1. Day   -   3-0 p.m. to 3-30 p.m.
                    Y.2. Day   -   3-30 p.m. to 4-0 p.m.

(4)   Heavy artillery bombardments will take place each day - but
        these will be without the co-operation of the Divisional
        Artillery.

(5)   There will be an intense bombardment by the Divisional
        Artillery daily, time to be notified later.

(6)   At -5 minutes all Wire Cutting Group less A/280 Battery
        (OBGUN) - will come under orders of Corps Artillery Counter
        Battery Group ; but C.R.A. Division will retain the right to
        call on two batteries in case of emergency.

(7)   After ZERO "Z" Day. The ammunition dumped at guns is not to
        fall below 500 rounds per gun 18 pdr. and 400 rounds per
        Howitzer 4.5".

                                (Signed) J.A. DON, Captain.
                        Brigade Major, R"A" 56th. Division .

Copy No.1 to PETART.
     2 to MACART.
     3 to SOART.
     4 to Divl. T. M. Officer.
     5 to X/56 T.M. Battery.
     6 to Y/56 T.M. Battery.
     7 to Z/56 T.M. BAttery.
     8 to V/56 T.M. Battery.
     9 to 56th. Division.
    10 to R.A. V11th. Corps.
    11 retained.
    12 retained.

SPECIAL 56th. DIVISIONAL ORDER.

The General Officer Commanding desires to express to all ranks his appreciation of the good work they have done during the past weeks, often under very adverse conditions. All ranks of all arms have co-operated to establish a completely new system of trenches, with all the necessary gun positions, observation posts, dug-outs, stores, aid posts and signal communications; and the heavy transport duties entailed in the provision of large quantities of material and stores have been most satisfactorily performed.

The Division is now about to have an opportunity of proving itself, to which the General Officer Commanding looks forward with complete confidence.

(Signed) J. BRIND. Lieut-Colonel
General Staff.

Headquarters. 56th. Division.
27th. June 1916.

Published to 281st. Brigade. R.F.A.

(Signed) C.C. MACDOWELL", Lt. Col
28th. June 1916.
Commanding 281st. Brigade. R.F.A.

SECRET.   I.D. 103.

The Operations ordered for "Z" DAY (to-morrow) are cancelled and the following substituted -:

"Y" 1 & 2 Days.

ALL BATTERIES.   Bombardment of Front line system, paying more
DURING DAY.   attention to the second & third lines and the
                  communication trenches thereto.

AMMUNITION.
                  109th. B. & C. Batteries - 380 H.E. 160 S.

                  "A" Battery.   - 360 H.E. 170 S.

                  "D" How's Battery.   - 100 H.E.

Y. 1. DAY.
                  From 4-40 p.m. to 5-15 p.m. there will be an
                  intense Bombardment of the front line system
                  by the Divisional Artillery, the bombardment increasing
                  in intensity during the last 10 minutes.
                       From 5-15 p.m. to 5-20 p.m. the Group
                  will lift on to the second line system, keeping
                  up the increased rate of fire.
                       At 5-20 p.m. the Group will return to the
                  front line system for 3 minutes at the slower rate
                  of fire and the bombardment will then cease.

AMMUNITION.
                  "A" Battery   -   215 H.E. 185 S.
                  "B" "   -   215 H.E. 190 S.
                  "C" "   -   255 H.E. 185 S.
                  "109th."   -   215 H.E. 100 S.
                  "D"   -   150 H.E.

Y. 2. DAY.
                  Scheme and Ammunition Allowance as for "Y" 1. DAY
                  but the times will be changed as follows :-

                       8-40 a.m.   -   9-15 a.m.
                       Lift 9-15 a.m.   to   9-20 a.m.
                       Return 9-29 a.m. for 3 minutes.

BY NIGHTS ON "Y" 1. & "Y" 2. DAYS.

                  Salvoes on Roads. trenches. tracks. selected points
                  and communication trenches -:
                       "A" Battery.   -   250 S.
                       "B" "   -   "
                       "C" "   -   "
                       "109th."   -   "
                       "D" "   -   50 H.E.

26/6/16.

                                                  Captain.
                                         Adjutant, MACART GROUP.

SECRET.   I.D. 108.

OPERATION ORDERS BY LT. COL. C. C. MACDOWELL, Commanding MACART GROUP.

NIGHT BEFORE "Z" DAY.

    On the night before "Z" day, Group Hdqrs. will move forward to dug-outs in MARDI TRENCH, arriving at 7-0 p.m.

SPECIAL DUTIES.

    This office letter I.D. No. 97 is cancelled and the following substituted on the night before "Z" day.

    Officers & telephonists will be detailed for duty as follows :—

F. O. O's.

    F. O. O. (Liaison) officer to be with the LONDON SCOTTISH and go forward to STRONG POINT when the infantry advance - Lt. G. B. WOLFE, one telephonist from each, ASHGUN & NICGUN, all fully equipped and with telephone, one mile of wire and 2 days' rations.

    F. O. O. (Liaison) officer to be with the RANGERS and go forward when the infantry advance - 2/Lt. J.A.E. FRIEND, two telephonists from FISHGUN, all fully equipped and with telephone, one mile of wire and 2 days' rations.

    These parties will report to Group Hdqrs. at 8-30 p.m. and will afterwards proceed to Hdqrs. of Infantry Battalion to which they are attached and advance with it if necessary.

    If called upon to establish independent communication with Group Hdqrs., it is intended that this should be done via Battn. Hdqrs. exchange and through new trenches dug in NO MAN'S LAND.

    F.O.O.'s will stay with Infantry Battn. until recalled, reporting to Group Hdqrs. all information obtainable.

    It is very important that no members of these parties should carry any maps or information likely to be of any use to the enemy.

O.P's.

    O.P. Control.   Lt. G.M. HAMILTON.
                          2/Lt. W.G. WHITE.
2 Hdqrs' telephonists with telephones, rations etc., also one telephonist from each, ASHGUN & NICGUN, with telephones, rations etc.

    O.P.H.   2/Lt. R. St. John CARR,
2 telephonists from FISHGUN with telephones etc.

    O.P.Z.   2/Lt. E. G. P. NATHAN & 2/Lt. W. G. FOWLER with 2 telephonists from JACKGUN and one from DYMHOW.

    O.P. Officers (and their telephonists) will be furnished with 3 days' rations and will be at their allotted O.P's by 8-0 p.m. and report to Group Headquarters. They will remain at the O.P. until further orders are received from Group Hdqrs. and report all information obtainable.

                                        Captain.
                          Adjutant, MACART GROUP.

SECRET.   I.D.

"Z" DAY before Zero Time.

Batt.	Time.	Operations.	AMM.
A.	(a) Before -65 minutes.	Bombardment of front line system and O.P.'s. Barrage of communication trenches.	150 H.E. 100 S.
	65 minutes(b) to Zero.	Intense bombardment of front line system.	800 H.E. 420 S.
"B"	Before (a) -65 minutes.	Same as for "A" Battery.	150 H.E. 100 S.
	65 minutes(b) to Zero.	Same as for "A" Battery.	800 H.E. 420 S.
"C"	Before (a) -65 minutes	Same as for "A" Battery.	150 H.E. 100 S.
	65 minutes(b) to Zero.	Same as for "A" Battery.	800 H.E. 420 S.
"D" HOW.	Before (a) -65 minutes.	Bombardment of front line system trench junctions	300 H.E.
	65 minutes(b) to Zero.	Intense bombardment of front line system trench junctions particularly EPTE.	1000 H.E.
109th.	Before (a) -65 minutes.	Same as for "A" Battery.	150 H.E. 100 S.
	65 minutes(b) to Zero.	Same as for "A" Battery. particularly EPTE.	800 H.E. 420 S.

281st Brigade RFA

War Diary for Month of July 1916

(ORIGINAL)

Army Form C. 2118

281 Brigade RFA
(of 1/2 London Brigade RFA)

WAR DIARY
or
INTELLIGENCE SUMMARY
(Erase heading not required.)

JULY 1916

Instructions regarding War Diaries and Intelligence Summaries are contained in F.S. Regs., Part II. and the Staff Manual respectively. Title Pages will be prepared in manuscript.

Place	Date	Hour	Summary of Events and Information	Remarks and references to Appendices
HEBUTERNE	1	Before 7.30 am	Intense & searching bombardment of enemy's trenches & strong points	
		After Zero (7.30am)	(Z day). Infantry attack on enemy's line as far as Southern group concerned London Scottish on right, Rangers on left. Both battalions of the 168th Brigade. 4th Division on right of 56th Division 169th Brigade did not take part in 1st attack, on the left the 169th Brigade moved to GOMMECOURT sector. Narrative of operations attached. Detail of operations attached	APPENDIX A Appendix B
			Batteries of Southern Group manned as follows: Col MacDOWELL commanding Group & enemy's 167th Infantry Brigade. A.B.C.D 281 Brigade C.D. 282 Brigade and C,B,+ 109E Batteries R.F.A	
SAILLY	4th	6pm		
	5th	6 am	Smoke discharge by infantry. 109th Battery and 282 C. Battery	

WAR DIARY
or
INTELLIGENCE SUMMARY

(Erase heading not required.)

July 1916   281st Brigade or Brigade R F A   Army Form C. 2118

Place	Date	Hour	Summary of Events and Information	Remarks and references to Appendices
SAILLY	6:	8am	Allotment of ammunition for wire cutting 250 rounds per battery	
"	7:	8 am	Smoke discharge by infantry repeated. All batteries bombardment of front line system 250 rounds per battery, 109th Battery & 282 C battery wire cutting 200 rounds per battery.	
	8:		C. 123 battery attached to the group	
	9:	6 am	Smoke discharge by infantry all batteries bombardment of enemy's front line system	
	10:		Regrouping of batteries Southern Group, namely A.B.C.D 281st Brigade B & C batteries 280 Brigade (now) 168th Infantry Brigade	
	13:	2.30 am	Brigade Wagon lines moved from HENU to PAS Group co-operated with Heavy Trench Mortars to cover the latters registration	

WAR DIARY / INTELLIGENCE SUMMARY

281st Brigade RFA

Army Form C.2118

JULY 1916

Place	Date	Hour	Summary of Events and Information	Remarks and references to Appendices
SAILLY	1st		Telegrams from the Commander in Chief	
	3rd		Letter from Corps Commander, 7th Corps, & GOC 56th Division	Appendix A
	15"		Letter from the Commander in Chief	Appendix B
	15"		Extracts from Report by GOC 168th Inf Brigade	Appendix C
	14"		280 B Battery leaves the southern group, which is now composed of 4- 18PR batteries & one 4.5 battery	
	15		One section C.281 & one section A.281 move for 24 hours into new cutting positions B 281 assisting in this operation	
	16		A raid took place by London Scottish & Kensingtons on enemy trenches with the object of capturing prisoners & otherwise. Raid/reverse attempt unsuccessful.	
	night		Bombardment by SOUTHERN GROUP commencing at 12 midnight. Ammunition 18PRS 250 rounds per battery. Hows 75 rds per battery	

WAR DIARY
or
INTELLIGENCE SUMMARY
(Erase heading not required.)

281st Brigade RFA

Army Form C. 2118

JULY 1916

Place	Date	Hour	Summary of Events and Information	Remarks and references to Appendices
SAILLY	17th and night		Bombardment by SOUTHERN GROUP of enemy trenches opposite. 18 PRs. 500 rds per battery, Hows 175 per battery	
	18th and night		Bombardment as above. 150 rds per battery	
HEBUTERNE NIGHT 8.9			Captain NICHOLLS commanding B battery 281 volunteered to go out and to bring in a wounded man which he had observed from his OP. This he did during the night 8th-9th finding two wounded men and carrying one of these right across into HEBUTERNE	
SAILLY	19th		Headquarters 281st Brigade move to HUTS PAS for next command handed over temporarily to Lt Col SOUTHAM 280 Brigade RFA who with his staff relieved the 281st Brigade	

Army Form C. 2118

WAR DIARY
or
INTELLIGENCE SUMMARY

JULY 1916   281 Brigade RFA

(Erase heading not required.)

Instructions regarding War Diaries and Intelligence Summaries are contained in F. S. Regs., Part II. and the Staff Manual respectively. Title Pages will be prepared in manuscript.

Place	Date	Hour	Summary of Events and Information	Remarks and references to Appendices
PAS.	20		Inspection by CO of Brigade Wagon lines. Lt Wolfe reported wounded at "A" battery OP.	
	29		Major JACKSON "C" battery proceeded to Field Ambulance. Lt HAMILTON "B" battery appointed to command "C" battery	
	29		School for Divisional Artillery Subalterns commenced at HUTS PAS. 1 officer per Brigade and OAC Kr LES Jackson to act as instructors in gunnery.	

appendix A

"Z" DAY AFTER

ZERO.

SECRET.   I.D. 103.

"BARRAGES A. BATTERY".

Time.	Operations.
At Zero. (a)	Direct on to FAME (BLUE BARRAGE)
Zero to +2 mins (b)	Intense bombardment for 2 minutes.
+2 to +4 " (c)	Lift on to GREEN BARRAGE up communication trenches ELBE & ANNA by 50 yd. increases.
+4 to +17 " (d)	Remain on GREEN BARRAGE
At +17 " (e)	YELLOW BARRAGE, lifting from communication trenches as mentioned below.

THE BARRAGES.

TRENCH BARRAGE of this Battery is the trench FATE.

BLUE BARRAGE of this Battery is the trench FAME.

GREEN BARRAGE of this Battery is from the intersection of the 140 contour with ELBE communication trench to point '03 (the intersection of ANNA with road) including the communication trench ELBE but not within 200 yards of its junction with FELON.

YELLOW BARRAGE is the same as GREEN BARRAGE but not including the communication trench.

RED BARRAGE is the same as the YELLOW.

NOTE. -:   RATE OF FIRE.

Up to GREEN BARRAGE, maximum rate.

From GREEN onwards : 1 round per gun per 30 seconds increasing or decreasing rate as situation requires.

SPECIAL NOTE.

Sponge out after every 30 rounds (18 pdrs)

SECRET.   I.D. 107.

"BARRAGES B BATTERY".

Time.   Operations.

Up to Zero.   (a) The first line trench FARMYARD.
Zero to +2 minutes (b) Lift on to BLUE BARRAGE up communication
                        trenches by 50 yd. increases, arriving at
                        +2 minutes.
+2 to +4   "   (c) Remain on BLUE BARRAGE.
At +4   "   (d) Lift on to GREEN BARRAGE.
+4 to +17   "   (e) Remain on GREEN BARRAGE.
At +17   "   (f) YELLOW BARRAGE, lifting from communication
                        trenches as mentioned below.

THE BARRAGES.

TRENCH BARRAGE of this Battery is the trench FARMYARD.

BLUE BARRAGE of this Battery is the trench FABLE, to the intersection of FABLE & ARUN.

GREEN BARRAGE of this Battery is from point '03 to the intersection of ARUN & FAST and the communication trenches ANNA & ANT, but not within 200 yards of their junction with FABLE.

YELLOW BARRAGE of this Battery is the same as the GREEN BARRAGE but not including the communication trenches.

RED BARRAGE is the same as the YELLOW BARRAGE.

RATE of FIRE.

Note.

Up to GREEN BARRAGE, maximum rate.

From GREEN onwards : 1 round per gun per 30 seconds.

Increasing or decreasing rate as situation requires.

Special Note.

Sponge out after every 20 rounds (18 pdrs)

SECRET.   I.D. 107.

"BARRAGES C BATTERY".

Time.	Operations.
Up to Zero.	(a) The front line trenches FAIR & FACE.
Zero to +2 mins.	(b) Lift on to ARUN TRENCH and remain on ARUN
+2 to +17 "	TRENCH throughout the whole of the operation.

THE BARRAGES.

TRENCH BARRAGE of this Battery are the trenches FAIR & FACE.

BLUE BARRAGE of this Battery is the trench ARUN from its intersection with FANCY to its intersection with FAST.

GREEN BARRAGE of this Battery is the same as the BLUE BARRAGE.

YELLOW BARRAGE is the same as the GREEN BARRAGE.

RED BARRAGE is the same as the YELLOW BARRAGE.

RATE of FIRE.

NOTE.

Up to GREEN BARRAGE : maximum rate.

From GREEN onwards : 1 round per gun per 30 seconds, increasing or decreasing rate as situation requires.

SPECIAL NOTE.   Sponge out after every 30 rounds (18 pdrs)

SECRET.   I.D. 107.

"BARRAGES D. HOW. BATTERY"

Time   Operation.

At & after Zero.   (a) 1st Section will deal exclusively with SUNKEN

                        ROAD from its junction with its

                        front line to K.11. d.50.05 and

                        remain on SUNKEN ROAD, throughout

                        all BARRAGES searching at irregular

                        intervals between these two points.

Time			
Up to Zero.	(a)	2nd. Section.	TRENCH BARRAGE.
Zero to +2 mins.	(b)	"	Lift on to BLUE BARRAGE. arriving +2 mins.
+2 to +4 "	(c)	"	Remain on BLUE BARRAGE.
At +4 "	(d)	"	Lift to GREEN BARRAGE.
+4 to +17 "	(e)	"	Remain on GREEN BARRAGE.
At +17 "	(f)	"	YELLOW BARRAGE.
At +30 "	(g)	"	RED BARRAGE.

THE BARRAGES.

HOWS' 1st. Section.

TRENCH BARRAGE	-	SUNKEN ROAD. as above.
BLUE BARRAGE.	-	" "
GREEN BARRAGE.	-	" "
YELLOW BARRAGE.	-	" "
RED BARRAGE.	-	" "

HOWS' 2nd Section.

TRENCH BARRAGE - Trench junctions in rear of STRONG POINT.

BLUE BARRAGE. - Intersection of ELBE & ET.

GREEN BARRAGE - Intersection of ARUN & FAST.

YELLOW BARRAGE.- Point '03.

RED BARRAGE - Intersection of EPTE & MESS.

Note.   RATE of FIRE.

Section Salvoes up to GREEN BARRAGE - maximum rate.

GREEN BARRAGE ditto.

YELLOW BARRAGE interval 30 seconds increasing or decreasing rate of fire as situation demands.

RED BARRAGE as for YELLOW BARRAGE returning to YELLOW or GREEN, if required.

SECRET.   J.D. 107.

"BARRAGES 109th. BATTERY"

Time.		Operations.
Up to Zero	(a)	The front line trench FETTER.
Zero to +2 minutes	(b)	Lift on to BLUE BARRAGE, arriving +2 minutes up communication trenches by 50 yd. increases.
+2 to +4 "	(c)	Remain on BLUE BARRAGE.
At +4 "	(d)	Lift on to GREEN BARRAGE.
+4 to +17 "	(e)	Remain on GREEN BARRAGE.
At +18 "	(f)	YELLOW BARRAGE lifting from communication trenches as mentioned below.

THE BARRAGES.

TRENCH BARRAGE of this Battery is FETTER.

BLUE BARRAGE of this Battery is the trench FELON.

GREEN BARRAGE of this Battery is from the intersection of EPTE & MESS to the intersection of the 140 contour with ELBE and the communication trench EPTE, but not within 300 yards of its junction with the 3rd. line trench FELON.

YELLOW BARRAGE of this Battery is as the GREEN BARRAGE including the communication trench EPTE but not within 300 yards of its junction with the 3rd. line trench FELON.

RED BARRAGE is as the YELLOW.

- RATE of FIRE. -

NOTE.

Up to GREEN BARRAGE : maximum rate.

From GREEN onwards : 1 round per per gun 30 seconds.

increasing or decreasing rate as situation requires.

SPECIAL NOTE.   Sponge out after every 20 rounds (18 pdrs)

Appendix B

The BOMBARDMENT.

On the morning of the 24th. June the Southern Group commenced a 7 days' bombardment on the German Front & Second line trench systems with their communication trenches ; co-operating day by day with the heavy artillery.

Under cover of the artillery fire the Infantry made trial Smoke attacks on W.X & Y days.

D/281 Howitzer Battery co-operated twice with the Heavy Group in bombarding BUCQUOY.

The days of the bombardment were expressed by the letters U. V. W. X. Y. Y.i. and Z (before Zero time) days.

The sector covered by the Group was from "NAMELESS FARM" on the North to SUNKEN ROAD on the South

The Southern was in touch on the left with the Northern Group.

The ATTACK.

The bombardment was in preparation for an Infantry advance on the enemy trenches from SUNKEN ROAD northward, joining up with the 46th. Division ; and having as its object the taking of the STRONG POINT in K.11.c. in our own sector, and GOMMECOURT PARK, WOOD & VILLAGE to the North.

The actual attack took place at 7-30 A.M. on "Z" day the 1st. July(expressed in the orders as Zero time) when our Infantry left the trenches under cover of smoke and accompanied by an intense bombardment of the enemy's front line trenches.

The attack was delivered by the London Scottish on the right and the Rangers on the left.

OBSERVATIONS from O.P. CONTROL.

The Infantry advanced by platoons from the head of each Battalion and gained the enemy front line trenches under cover of smoke. The smoke seemed to be , from observation, rather in front of the Infantry than around them. They appeared to suffer but few casualties from rifle fire but the enemy's Shrapnel was effective undoubtedly, from the number of men seen to fall.

They gained the enemy's front line trenches without difficulty however ; but on reaching which, they were shelled by the enemy with great determination both with 77 m.m. 4'2 & 5'9.

At the same time our front & second line trenches & communication trenches were dealt with by 4'2s & 5'9s followed by sharp bursts of Shrapnel.

The London Scottish appeared to gain the whole of their objective and bombing could be seen on both flanks.

The enemy's Infantry massed in considerable numbers in FAIR, FACE , FANCY many of them getting on top of the parapet to shoot at our men in the STRONG POINTS; C Battery dealt most effectively with them and the enemy undoubtedly suffered considerable loss.

The Rangers on the left of the London Scottish made good the enemy's trenches FETTER, FATE and from there were seen to gain the second line trenches FELT & FALL.

Working up ELBE to point 16 they turned to the left up FELON and gained the trenches about NAMELESS FARM. When they reached this point a strong force of the enemy was seen rushing down the EPTE trench , which trench was seen to be thickly held.

Fire of D/281 & 109th. Batteries were directed upon it and after some small correction was made in the fire of both these batteries from the Control O.P. shells from both of these could be observed falling direct into the enemy's trench and men could be seen both scrambling and blown out of this trench

All further advance was observed to be checked down EPTE.

At the same time the communication trenches ELBE, FABLE, ANT & ANNA were dealt with to prevent movement of the enemy.

As far as observation could tell both the Rangers & London Scottish appeared to gain their objectives but were unable to hold them owing to the intense artillery fire fire brought to bear on all the trenches of the system.

It is very difficult to say but I do not think that the enemy's bombers advanced in any force.

Two strong detachments, one of the London Scottish and one of the Rangers were seen to go out carrying bombs & ammunition ; only one or two men of each detachment reached the enemy's line owing to his intense Shrapnel Barrage across "No Man's Land" and to a certain amount of rifle & machine gun fire from the SUNKEN ROAD direction.

Parties of our Infantry were seen coming from GOMMECOURT VILLAGE and strong numbers of the enemy Infantry were seen working down EXE & EMS.

The retirement of the Rangers from the trench junctions in EPTE appeared to be commencing and violent bombing could be seen at EPTE junction with FELON and EPTE junction with FELL ; but their retirement across "No Man's Land" was not seen. The London Scottish however mounting to parapet in two parties of about 100 each, could be seen moving across "No Man's Land" in the direction of BRICKYARD, the last party followed by about 150 Germans who climbed up on the parapet and shot upon our men.

An intense fire was brought to bear on the strong point by "B" Battery and it appeared to be effective for the HUNS disappeared ; many killed being seen lying on the parapet.

Rifle fire from SUNKEN ROAD and machine gun fire from the same front caused many casualties to the London Scottish in its retirement and they were met when they reached our front line by an intense barrage, SHRAPNEL & 4'2s.

During the whole of the attack the enemy heavily barraged our front line system in W. sector both the new and the old line and the communication trenches ; their fire was incessant and appeared to be an organised searching by Batteries or Groups ; there was no rifle fire on our trenches.

Throughout the whole of the operations it was very difficult to observe, owing to the smoke & dust caused by the enemy's barrages.

One Battery of the enemy's artillery was observed to come into action, during the operations near ROSSIGNOL WOOD - the teams were seen.

Some officers were observed, whilst the London Scottish were retiring, standing in front of the trees of ROSSIGNOL WOOD ; one of the party was carrying a flag ; they disappeared on being fired upon by the Howitzer Battery.

At the later stage small formed parties of the enemy could be seen advancing at intervals down the road between ROSSIGNOL WOOD and the Crucifix ; these were dealt with by our artillery and were observed to break up and disappear.

GENERAL DEDUCTIONS.

Principal casualties were undoubtedly caused by Shrapnel and high explosives; they appeared to suffer very little at any time from Rifle fire.

The enemy's barrages on "No Man's Land" rendered the reinforcement of our troops, both as regards ammuntion and men in the enemy's trenches - even if reinforcements were available - practically impossible.

The number of the enemy Batteries appeared to increase as the day wore on, and the barrages undoubtedly increased in intensity.

It is a fact worthy of notice that the enemy during the attack appeared to direct nearly all his fire on the Infantry and on our trench systems, rather than on our Batteries.

Macdonnell

LIEUT. COLONEL
COMMANDING 251 BRIGADE,
ROYAL FIELD ARTILLERY.

Appendix C

The following telegram was received on the night of July 1st/1916.

"THE COMMANDER-IN-CHIEF SENT HIS A.D.C. TO CONGRATULATE THE DIVISION ON ITS FINE WORK TO-DAY.

HE SAYS THAT OWING TO THE GALLANT ATTACK OF THE 30th. DIVISION THE 8th. CORPS WERE ENABLED TO CAPTURE SHIRE."

7th Corps G.C.R.237/140.　　　　　　　　　　　56th Divn. S.G.121/79.

56th Division.

    The Corps Commander wishes to congratulate all ranks of the 56th Division on the way in which they took the German trenches and held them by pure grit and pluck for so long in very adverse circumstances.

    Although GOMMECOURT has not fallen into our hands, the purpose of the attack, which was mainly to contain and kill Germans, was accomplished, thanks to a great extent to the tenacity of the 56th Division.

                           Sgd/ F. Lyon, Brigadier-General,

3rd July, 1916.　　　　　　　　　　General Staff, VIIth Corps.

- 2 -

....

    Forwarded.　The General Officer Commanding the 56th Division wishes all ranks to know how proud he is of the splendid way in which they captured the German trenches, and of the way they held on to them until all their ammunition and grenades were exhausted.

    He is satisfied that the main task of the Division in containing and killing Germans was most thoroughly accomplished.

Hdqrs. 56th Divn.　　　　　　　　　　　　　Lieut. Colonel,

3rd July, 1916.　　　　　　　　　　　　　　General Staff.

Third Army No. S.G.R.46/2.   56th Division S.G.121/96
VIIth Corps G.C.R.233/182.

General Officer Commanding

Third Army.

O.A.D.64.

The Commander-in-Chief directs me to confirm in writing the verbal message already delivered by an A.D.C. to General SNOW, conveying his appreciation of the gallant efforts made at GOMMECOURT on the 1st and 2nd July by the 46th and 56th Divisions of the VIIth Corps.

While deeply deploring the losses suffered by these Divisions he is glad to be able to assure them that their vigorous and well-sustained attack has proved of material assistance to the success of the general plan of operations.

Adv. G.H.Q.   (sd.) L.E.KIGGELL,
                                          Lieut-General,
13th July, 1916.   Chief of the General Staff.

2.

VIIth Corps.

The Army Commander forwards with pleasure, the above letter from the Chief of the General Staff.

15th July, 1916.   (sd.) L.J.BOLS, Maj.Gen.
                              General Staff, Third Army.

3.

. . . .

Forwarded for communication to all ranks.

Head Qrs. 56th Divn.   Lieut-Colonel,
17th July, 1916.   General Staff.

56th. Division. S.G. 181/01.

C. R. A.

    56th. Division.

Appendix C

       The following extracts from a report on the operations of 1st. July by 168th. Infantry Brigade on Artillery Co-operation is forwarded for your information

    "A Group of 4. 18 pdr. Batteries and one 4'5" Howitzer Battery was affiliated to the Brigade under Lieut. Colonel MACDOWELL, R.F.A. This officer and his staff occupied Battle Headquarters with me and from him I received all day the greatest support. The closest touch with all Batteries was maintained throughout the entire operation, and to this, coupled with the valuable observation from O.P.'s and R.A. Officer at my headquarters I attribute the great support it was possible to give to the infantry.

    To illustrate this more closely - it was actually possible to see the struggle of our infantry in the German Lines, to put guns on to such trenches as were stopping their advance and to barrage others to the flanks, one occasion when German bombers in large number were clearly seen advancing down EPTE trench our Howitzers were put on and at the second salvo completely checked the movement, killing several Germans by a direct hit in the trench (observed from Brigade H.Q.) "

                         (Signed) J. BRIND ,
                                Lieut-Colonel,
14-7-16.   General Staff, 56th. Division.

---

(2)

Lieut. Colonel C.C. MACDOWELL,

    Commanding 281st. Brigade, R.F.A.

        For retention.

                          (Signed) J. H. DON, Major,
15-7-16.   Brigade-Major, R. A. 56th. Division.

56th Divisional Artillery.

281st BRIGADE

ROYAL FIELD ARTILLERY.

AUGUST 1 9 1 6

AUGUST 1916.

WAR DIARY
or
INTELLIGENCE SUMMARY

281 Brigade
RFA (late 1/2 LONDON)

Army Form C. 2118

Place	Date	Hour	Summary of Events and Information	Remarks and references to Appendices
SAILLY	6		Vicinity of A battery shelled. Major Abel Smith wounded in the head and evacuated to Field Ambulance	
"	7		There was not much activity during the past week. Our four (4) battrie dead horses with working parties, hostile machine guns etc	
			R.J.F.S. Jackson assumes temporarily command of A battery	
"	9		No. 996 Bmbr Cottis and 1547 Gunner Fearn both of A battery presented with the ribbon of the Military Medal for gallantry in the field by the GOC 56th Division	
"	14		Slight increase of activity in both our own and the enemy's artillery. The GOC RA VII Corps Br/Gen Ross Johnson inspected the OPs of the group & expressed himself extremely pleased with the work put in on the OPs themselves, their situation and with the liaison system, a central exchange system used in the Southern Group	

Army Form C. 2118

WAR DIARY
or
INTELLIGENCE SUMMARY

(Erase heading not required.)

AUGUST 1916 281 Brigade RFA

Instructions regarding War Diaries and Intelligence Summaries are contained in F. S. Regs., Part II and the Staff Manual respectively. Title Pages will be prepared in manuscript.

Place	Date	Hour	Summary of Events and Information	Remarks and references to Appendices
SAILLY	15th		Both our batteries & the enemy's still active	
"	18		SAILLY Group Headquarters shelled with 4.3" TT's from direction of PUISIEUX. South Group in cooperation with Heavy Artillery shelled BUCQUOY wire with accuracy	
	19th		SAILLY again shelled. Relief of 56th Division by 17th Division commenced in this Brigade area. 505 Hy Brigade (Brig Gen Glasgow) relieving 168 Hy Brigade (Brig Gen Kock CMG)	APPENDIX A
	20th		SAILLY & Group HQrs again shelled, whole Hy 17th Division completed	
	21st		SAILLY & Group HQrs shelled twice during the day. enemy's artillery active throughout the day. Captain & Adjt Rea took over command of A Battery	
	22nd		W/C Sing appointed Battery adjutant	

WAR DIARY or INTELLIGENCE SUMMARY

Army Form C. 2118

281 Brigade RFA

AUGUST 1916

Place	Date	Hour	Summary of Events and Information	Remarks and references to Appendices
SAILLY	28th		Activity of enemy artillery, machine guns and trench mortar has been gradually increasing during the last week. NEBUTERNE, SAILLY and the plain between these villages receiving considerable attention. SOUTHERN GROUP co-operating with Northern & Centre Falk part in an offensive shoot on Rettemoy Farm area.	
			The section of each battery viewed by one section 79th Brigade RFA 17th Division. Sections of 281st Brigade proceed to PAS HUTS. Relief completed by midnight with casualties. Registration by sections of 79th Brigade in return.	B
	29th		Southern Group come under orders of 17th Division.	
	30th		Personal Headquarters HENU	
	31st		Remaining sections of 281st Brigade RFA relieved by 79th Brigade 17th Division. Relieved sections proceeded from battery positions to PAS HUTS.	C

LIEUT. COLONEL
Commanding 281 Brigade,
Royal Field Artillery.

7th Corps G.S. 1044. 56th Divn.
G.241.

A

56th Division.

The Lieutenant-General Commanding VIIth Corps in saying good-bye to the 56th Division on their leaving the Corps, desires to record his appreciation of the manner in which the Division has fought and worked while it has been in the VIIth Corps. The gallant manner in which the Division fought at GOMMECOURT will be appreciated in history, but the Corps Commander wishes the Division to know that the less spectacular but more irksome work which the Division has put into the line which they have been holding, has not escaped notice. It is invidious to make distinction when all have worked so well, but he particularly congratulates those units who have so well repaired that part of the line knocked about in the fighting on 1st July.

The Corps Commander wishes all ranks good luck and feels sure that any task committed to the Division in the future will be completed in triumph.

Sgd/ F. LYON, Brigadier-General,
19th August, 1916.   General Staff, VIIth Corps.

SECRET.   B   O.O. No. 120.

OPERATION ORDERS BY LT. COL. C. C. MACDOWELL, Commanding SOUTHERN GROUP,
50th. Div. Artillery.

(1) A Section of the following Batteries will be relieved to-night August 30th., by sections of 17th. Divisional Artillery :-

{ ALL BATTERIES, SOUTHERN GROUP.

B/ass Battery, NORTHERN GROUP.

C/283.}
D/250.} Batteries, Centre Group.

(2) On the night of Thursday 31st. inst., the relief of all Batteries of which one section was relieved on the night of 28th. inst., will be completed by 17th. Divisional Artillery.

(3) Command of Southern Group and of Batteries of all Groups whose relief is completed on the night August 31st/September 1st will be assumed by relieving Group and Battery Commanders, 17th. Divisional Artillery, at 10.0. A.M. on September 1st.

(4) In all cases Sections, 17th. Divisional Artillery, will not move East of the line M. ALAND-SQUATRE before 7.45.P.M.

(5) Outgoing Sections will, on relief, proceed to their Wagon Lines.

(6) Instructions concerning ammunition will follow.

(7) Acknowledge.

August 30/16.

Acting Adjutant.
Southern Group, 50th. Div. Art.

SECRET.   I.D. No. 166.

OPERATION ORDERS BY LT. COL. C. C. MACDOWELL, Commanding SOUTHERN
            GROUP, 56th. Div. Artillery.

Further to above orders :-

(8)   Relieving Section will arrive at Battery Positions to-night
        the 28th. inst., at the following times :-

                ASHGUN by Section C/80, as arranged.
                BRAGUN by Section B/79 at 10.0 P.M.
                JACKGUN by Section C/79 at 11.0 P.M.
                NICGUN by Section A/79 at 12.0 P.M.
                DYMHOW by Section D/79, as arranged at 1.0 A.M.

        Teams of relieving sections will withdraw Guns and take them
        to the Wagon Lines of relieving Batteries at GAUDIEMPRE.
        Battery Commanders will arrange for their own limbers and teams
        to take Guns on from there to Wagon Lines at PAS.

(9)   Guides to meet relieving sections at Fork Roads :-
        BAYENCOURT - COIGNEUX - SAILLY (Map Reference : J. 18.a.1.6.)
                            in good time
(10)   Right Sections will relieve unless otherwise arranged.

                                        W G White
                                        Acting Adjutant.
                                        Southern Group, 56th. Div. Art.

August 28/16.

SECRET.

Further to I.D. No. 167, Dated August 30th/16.
----

(9) Relief of Remaining Sections will take place at the
     following times on the evening of the 31st. inst.

     C/79 Brigade will relieve JACKGUN at 8-0.P.M.

     C/80 Brigade will relieve ASIGUN at 9-30.P.M.

     B/79 Brigade will relieve BRAGUN at 10-0.P.M.

     A/79 Brigade will relieve NIGGUN at 10-30.P.M.

     D/79 Brigade will relieve DIMBOW at 11-30.P.M.

(10) Battery Commanders will make their own arrangements for the
     relieving teams to take out the sections relieved back to
     GAUDIEMPRE and for their own Teams to take them from there
     to the Wagon Line at PAS.

August 30th/16.

                                    D. M'K1b
                                    Acting Adjutant,
                                 381st. Brigade, R.F.A.

SECRET. Copy No.

OPERATION ORDERS No. 167 by Lt. Col. C. C. MACDOWELL,
Commanding 281st. Brigade. R.F.A.

August 30th/16.

MOVE.

(1) The Move of the 281st. Brigade, R.F.A. will take place as follows :-

Night 31st. August/1st. Sept. Relief of remaining Sections of Batteries.

Sept. 1st. (10.0.A.M.) Relief of Group & Battery Commands.

September 2nd. PAS HUTS to MEZEROLLES via POMMERA and DOULLENS.

September 3rd. MEZEROLLES to VITZ-VILLEROY.

---

(2) The Brigade will rendezvous, head of the column at BEAUREPAIRE at 9-45 A.M. on September 2nd.

The Brigade on assembling will move in the following order :-
Headquarters. "B" "A" "C" "D"

All G.S. Wagons, Cooks' Carts and Officers' Mess Carts will be closed up in rear of their respective Batteries.

The distance between Batteries on the march will be 25 yards.

(3) Officers Commanding Batteries are reminded that all vehicles must be clear of DOULLENS by 11-30. A.M.

(4) Halts at 10 minutes to the hour (The column will not halt in DOULLENS)

(5) Supplies will be sent to Units at Half Way Billets by A.S.C.

(6) Billetting parties will be as follows :- Lt. WILSON and one cyclist per Battery to MEZEROLLES.
2/Lt. ESDAILE and one mounted N.C.O. per Battery and H.Q.S. with horseholders to VITZ-VILLEROY.
The Interpreter will accompany Lt. WILSON and assist him in arranging billets at MEZEROLLES and will afterwards proceed to VITZ-VILLEROY and report to 2/Lt. ESDAILE.
Billetting parties should arrive 24 hours in advance at both the half way and final billets.

(7) The H.Q. of the 56th. Div. Artillery will be at ST. RIQUIER.

(8) Acknowledge

Acting Adjutant,
281 t. Brigade, R.F.A.

Copy No. 1 to 56th. Div. Art.
2 A/281 Battery.
3 B/281   "
4 C/281   "
5 D/281   "
6 281st. Bde. Wagon Line.
7 & 8 Retained.

56th Divisional Artillery.

281st (late 2nd London) BRIGADE R.F.A.

SEPTEMBER 1916.

SEPTEMBER 1916

WAR DIARY or INTELLIGENCE SUMMARY

Army Form C.2118

281st Brigade RFA

Lt Col 2/1 London Brigade RFA

Place	Date	Hour	Summary of Events and Information	Remarks and references to Appendices
PAS.	1st		Relief of Group and Battery Commanders at SALLY AU BOIS by 17th Divisional Artillery (79th Brigade RFA) Brigade HQrs moved to PAS HUTS	
OUTRE BOIS	2nd		Brigade marched to OUTREBOIS there to be billeted.	
RAINE VILLE	3rd 4th		Brigade marched to RAINNEVILLE. "	
DAOURS	5th		Brigade marched to DAOURS near CORBIE then bivouacked	
BRAY	6th		Brigade marched to BRAY-SUR-SOMME then bivouacked	
	7th		OC + Battery Commanders reconnoitred area about GUILLEMONT and HARDECOURT	
	8th		OC took over command of 281st Brigade RFA which moved forward into position E of HARDECOURT	
	9th		Bombardment to support infantry attack on LEUSE WOOD	
	10th		Situations continued	
	11th		OC taking 281st Brigade in position in WEDGE WOOD Valley 6 am.	

Army Form C 2118

WAR DIARY
or
INTELLIGENCE SUMMARY
(Erase heading not required.)

Instructions regarding War Diaries and Intelligence Summaries are contained in F.S. Regs., Part II. and the Staff Manual respectively. Title Pages will be prepared in manuscript.

Place	Date	Hour	Summary of Events and Information	Remarks and references to Appendices
HARDE-COURT	12th		The Group consisted of A.281, B.281, B.280, C.280, D.280, D.281. In position HARDECOURT ANGLE WOOD VALLEY WEDGE WOOD VALLEY in support of the 281st Brigade	
	13th		Heavy fire went advanced of any batteries in action. Reputation preparing to attack. The group supported the attack of the Guards Division on the Quadrilateral near GINCHY. Attack taking place between 6 am & 6 pm	
	14th		We within by A.M.S. batteries in front of MORVAL continued throughout the night. Captain GRAY wounded. While in command of the A.281 Battery. Captain A.V. REID Heavy Trench Mortar Battery 56th Division temporarily takes command of A.281.	
	15th		Bombardment of enemy's position near MORVAL. Bombardment of enemy's position about BOULEAUX WOOD and MORVAL by 56th Division 6th Division and Guards Division Artillery	

WAR DIARY
or
INTELLIGENCE SUMMARY

(Erase heading not required.)

Army Form C. 2118

Place	Date	Hour	Summary of Events and Information	Remarks and references to Appendices
HARDECOURT	15"	6.20 am	Operations commenced & continued all day results indecisive.	
	16"		Bombardment of enemy positions continued. Grenade Division made a further attack on the Quadrilateral which were successful.	
	17"		Nile cutting in front of MORVAL. Op. in front of LEUSE WOOD being used.	
	18"		Bombardment commenced 5.50 am in support of an attack by 167" Brigade on BOULEAUX WOOD	
	19"	4-6 pm	MACDOWELL GROUP consisting of A & B 281, D 281 & B 280 came under 6" Division	
	20"		B 280 moved from old position to an advanced one in WEDGE WOOD VALLEY. Heavy bombardment of our battery positions 2/Lt POWELL and 2 Sergeants wounded & 2 gunners killed	

WAR DIARY
or
INTELLIGENCE SUMMARY

Army Form C 2118

Place	Date	Hour	Summary of Events and Information	Remarks and references to Appendices
	21st		Wire cutting carried out by A & B 281. and B 280 in front of MORVAL. B 281 heavily shelled by the enemy following officers wounded. Lt Jackson. Lt COLE (killed) 2nd Lt MARSDEN 2nd Lt BURNS. 2nd Lt WHITE (killed)	
	22nd		C. 281. joined group in place of B 280 C. 281 moved to forward position in WEDGEWOOD VALLEY Wire cutting continued during the enemy	
	23rd		Preliminary bombardment in preparation for general attack of MORVAL	
	24th	8am	Bombardment of MORVAL continued & wire cutting	
	25th		Bombardment continued during the morning 12.30 pm Attack on MORVAL by the 95th Inf Brigade operations successful. MORVAL reoccupied about 6 pm. Lt BLUMER (killed) carrying out a reconnaissance	

SEPTEMBER

WAR DIARY
or
INTELLIGENCE SUMMARY

(Erase heading not required.)

Army Form C 2118

Place	Date	Hour	Summary of Events and Information	Remarks and references to Appendices
HARDECOURT	26th		COMBLES Taken by the 56th Division & FRENCH Troops	
	27th		Brigadier General ELKINGTON CMG assumed command of 56th Division which freed the Right Centre Group Rifles	
			Outlying OP's established in front of MORVAL	
	28th	9.30	A B C & D batteries moved forward & gained SW of MORVAL by 8.30am all batteries were in action	
			Registration continued, all battery positions under heavy Shell fire from the direction of SAILLY-SAILLISEL	
	29th		1 Officer wounded 4 other ranks killed 6 wounded	
			Enemy bombardment of hostile areas in direction of LE TRANSLOY	
	30th		On retreat of MORVAL & battery positions continued under heavy shell fire	

SEPTEMBER WAR DIARY or INTELLIGENCE SUMMARY

Army Form C. 2118

281 Brigade RFA 2nd London Brigade T.F.

Place	Date	Hour	Summary of Events and Information	Remarks and references to Appendices
HARDECOURT	30		During the operations terminating with the capture of MORVAL the 281st Brigade were in the greater portion of the time, apparently the most advanced of Brigades of Artillery in the offensive. The total casualties for the month were 4 killed or died, 6 officers wounded, 6 other ranks killed 19 other ranks wounded. The attached complimentary letters were received. (1) from Major General Stephens 5th Division (2) G.O.C. RA XIV Corps (3) G.O.C. XIV Corps (4) Major General Hull 56th Division	A B C D

Churchill
Lieut. Colonel
Commanding 281st Bde R.F.A.

A   No. B.M. 946.

Right Group.
Left Group.

 Major-General STEPHENS, Commanding the 5th Division, has expressed his thanks to the Officers, Non-Commissioned Officers and men of the Royal Artillery for their spendid work yesterday, and adds that it is in great measure due to their good arrangements and untiring labours that the Infantry were able to gain a brilliant success.

 The C. R. A. desires that the above may be made known to all ranks and to congratulate them on receiving such high praise, which they have so fully merited.

            Major, R. A.
26/9/16.   Brigade Major, Right Centre Artillery.

6

B

Will look in [illegible] time

The following letter has been received

"The G.O.C, R.A. [illegible], to day phoned
"[with] the [southern] part of the
"[illegible] Artillery [illegible] I also [illegible]
"also with the very accurate and
"concise reports sent in by [you].
"Brig. General Ellington has asked
"me to say how gratified he is
"with the [work] done."

signed
A W [Ruckhle]
Lt Col R.A.
Commanding
R. Centre Arty.

16.9.16

"A" Form.
Army Form C. 2121.

MESSAGES AND SIGNALS.

Prefix .... Code .... m.	Words	Charge	This message is on a/c of:	Recd. at 6.36 p.m.
Office of Origin and Service Instructions.	Sent		................Service.	Date ....
	At .... m.			From ....
	To			
....	By		(Signature of "Franking Officer.")	By ....

TO —— All Units

Sender's Number.	Day of Month	In reply to Number.	AAA
H 7 12	25th	—	

Corps Commander wires again aaa Hearty thanks and sincere congratulations to you all aaa a very fine achievement splendidly executed aaa Ends.

From: Right Group
Place:
Time:

The above may be forwarded as now corrected.   (Z)

Censor. Signature of Addressor or person authorised to telegraph in his name.
* This line should be erased if not required.

56th. Division G. 932.

1. I have just come back from a conference with the Corps Commander at which he said that, the Commander-in-chief, the Army Commander and he himself fully appreciated the great work done by the XIVth. Corps, and the hard time they had gone through. He said that it was well known to the Germans that what was beating them was the grit and staying power of the British Soldier, and he called for one more effort on the part of the Corps to give the enemy a knock out blow which would bring us to our final objective.

2. The 56th. Division has done its part and done it well, they have had a trying time, and now the weather has turned against us too, but I am confident that we can be relied on to show a bold front, and that every officer and man will do his utmost when the time comes.

3. The enemy are worse off than ourselves especially in the matter of men and now is the time to strike him a crippling blow.

4. I wish all Commanding Officers to make these facts known to all ranks, and in conjunction with their officers, to impress on the men that during the next few days all must put their last ounce into the fight and any necessary work that has to be done.

Headquarters. 56th. Division. (Signed) C. HULL,
18th. September 1916. Major General,
Commanding 56th. Division.

The G.O.C., R.A. has every confidence in the keen-ness and readiness for personal self-sacrifice of all ranks. He wishes however to warn all ranks beforehand that the calls which will be made on them during the next ten days will be unprecedented. It is expected that every Officer and man will willingly work to the limit of his capacity, and, regardless of fatigue, ordinary procedure or danger.

The demands which will undoubtedly be made on men, horses and material will tax everyone to the uttermost, but with the determination to go all out, results more than repaying the effort will be ensured.

(Signed) J.A. DON, Major,
Brigade Major, R.A. 56th. Division.

Copies to all Brigades and Batteries.)
        Divl. Ammunition Column.)   56th. Divnl. Artillery.
        Trench Mortar Batteries.)

APPENDIX VII

Army Form C. 2118

WAR DIARY
or
INTELLIGENCE SUMMARY

(Erase heading not required.)

November 1916   169th Brigade
                 1st & London Brigade R.F.A.

Place	Date	Hour	Summary of Events and Information	Remarks and references to Appendices
BARLY COURT	1st		Relief of one section R.E. battery by one section B.F. Divisional Ammunition...	
	2nd		Relief of remaining sections by B. Divisional Column...	
			...weather conditions most difficult...	
			...until the second detachment...	
HAZEL ?	3rd		...Gun battle of HAZEL LINE B. ? advanced to E. KEBREW DADURE DOM BURTON...	
			...moved to KEREWIETE were billeted...	
KEREWIETE	4th		Brigade received word that move... gun... between A + B and B + C...	
	5th		...of the Brigade...	

WAR DIARY

Army Form C. 2118

November 1916

281st Brigade
1/10 LONDON Brigade RFA

INTELLIGENCE SUMMARY
(Erase heading not required.)

Place	Date	Hour	Summary of Events and Information	Remarks and references to Appendices
RIBEAUVILLE	5th		Officers made — Captain R.T. LEE to command A battery. Major G.L. DYMOTT to command B battery. Captain G.M. HAMILTON to command D battery. Orders received that 56th Divisional Artillery are to move this a.m. to the Line of once to relieve the 60th Divisional Artillery now on the St Canadian Division Corps runway to St VAAST. NEUVILLE ST VAAST.	
RIBEAUVILLE	6th		Brigade H.Q. moved forward to advanced Group H.Q. at BERTHONVAL FARM all batteries moved forward to positions with A&Q. and FREVIN CAPELLE. 56th Divisional Headquarters established at AUBIGNY	
BERTHONVAL FARM	7th		Relief of 60th Divisional Artillery by 56th Divisional Artillery completed at 2811 Brigade employing the Left Group of CANADIAN CORPS. with batteries in positions at LA TARGETTE and NEUVILLE ST VAAST	

NOVEMBER 1916 Brigade

WAR DIARY or INTELLIGENCE SUMMARY

Army Form C. 2118.

98th (S) Brigade R.F.A.

(Erase heading not required.)

Instructions regarding War Diaries and Intelligence Summaries are contained in F. S. Regs., Part II. and the Staff Manual respectively. Title pages will be prepared in manuscript.

Place	Date	Hour	Summary of Events and Information	Remarks and references to Appendices
BRUAY	8th		104" Battery bivouacked at the 98th Brigade Wagon lines at St Hilaire. News of a new A.104 Battery known to the brigade	
	10th		Negotiations with D.A. Battalion Little Wallets Uniform. Batmen orderlies & cyclists obtained by Brigade officers	
	15th		Inspection of Brigade by M.G.R.A. XI Corps at FREVIN CAPELLE accompanied by G.R.A. 56 Division	
	16th		Lord ROBERTS on the hunt	
	17th		Lt. HARDWELL (Pioneer) proceed to U.K. on leave	
	21st		Major FISHER resumed command of 98 Brigade	
	22nd		2nd Lieut. DULL invalided to hospital. No particulars known	
	25th 28th		Routine several trek route talks. The 56 Division (Artillery) under orders to proceed to XIV Corps	Letters from C.R.A. 56 Div Arty & M.G.R.A. XIV Corps A & B

T-2131. Wt. W708—76. 500000. 4/15. Sir J. C. & S.

CC

G. O. C., R.A.,
XlVth. Corps.
749.   25.10.16.

56th Divisional Artillery.

   The evidence of the Infantry of the 4th & 8th. Divisions is unanimous and conclusive that the 18 pdr. and 4.5" Howitzer Barrage on the 23rd, instant was quite excellent.

   The Corps Commander heartily congratulates all the Divisional Artillery concerned, fully realising the difficulties of location of enemy's trenches and our own.

      (Signed)   A. H. BARTHOLOMEW.
             Major.
25.10.16.   Staff Officer, R.A. XlVth. Corps.

Copy of telegram received on October 29th/16.

TO LUCRE.

   Following from LANSDOWNE begins:-
General PINNEY and LANSDOWNE thank you for your successful shooting yesterday.

COPY.

Now that the 56th Divisional Artillery has resumed normal Trench Warfare I would like you to let your Officers and men know how much I appreciated the work they did during the two months on the SOMME. Their shooting was uniformly excellent, and was acknowledged to be so by all the Divisions whom they covered. Both the Brigadier General R.A. XIVth. Corps and the C's.R.A. of the 4th and 6th Divisional Artilleries under whom the 56th Divisional Artillery at times worked, made complimentary remarks on the information sent back by F.O.O's. which reflects credit on both the officers and the signallers concerned.

I would like particularly to mention that the continuous hard work involved in ammunition supply is realised, and the uncomplaining spirit shown by officers and men, up to the end, in spite of long hours and trying weather conditions, fully appreciated.

I have told the Major-General Commanding R.A. First Army that I feel proud to command the 56th Divisional Artillery and that their work has been excellent throughout.

The M.G. R.A. First Army proposes to inspect the Divisional Artillery in the course of a few days and I have every confidence that when he does so he will find that the same spirit which was shewn on the SOMME, will shew itself in the efforts made to turn out horses, harness and equipment in such a way as to uphold the reputation of the 56th. Divisional Artillery.

(Signed) R. J. G. ELKINGTON,
Brigadier General,
10.11.16.   Commanding Royal Artillery, 56th Div.

To Lt. Col. C. C. MACDOWELL,
    281st Brigade, R. F. A.

281st. Bde. R.F.A.

War Diary for December 1916

ORIGINAL

WAR DIARY

281st Brigade RFA
(OC 1/2 LONDON BRIGADE RFA)

DECEMBER 1916

Place	Date	Hour	Summary of Events and Information
BERTHONVAL / ST ELOI	1st		All batteries 281st Brigade RFA relieved by 3rd Canadian Artillery and moved to wagon lines ACQ and CAPELLE FERMONT. Headquarters move to ACQ.
ACQ	2nd		The Brigade marched to area AUCHEL - RAINBERT via LES 4 VENTS and DIVION
RAINBERT 3rd / HAVERSKERQUE 4th			The Brigade continued the march to HAVERSKERQUE. Brigade commander proceeded to LAVANTIE to reconnoitre positions
	5th		Section relieved Section of the 6th Divisional in the line Remaining sections relieved all batteries of the Brigade in action as under LAVENTIE forming LEFT GROUP 56th DA Wagon lines established at LA GORGUE. LEFT GROUP consists of A 281 B281 D281 B280 + D280. Group Headquarters in LAVANTIE English sections B281 and B280 at PETILLON
	8th		Colonel MACDOWELL returned from leave and resumed command

DECEMBER 1916

28th Brigade
RFA
1st B = LONDON BRIGADE RFA

WAR DIARY
or
INTELLIGENCE SUMMARY.

ORIGINAL

Army Form C. 2118.

Place	Date	Hour	Summary of Events and Information	Remarks and references to Appendices
LAVANTIE	8th		Registration continued by all batteries. Little hostile activity hurt - very quiet, a great of wastes in trenches. Telephone communications bad. Battery positions wants a great deal of work put in items & repairs. Alternative positions in a bad state. OP's good but observation poor owing to weather conditions.	
	9th		23550 Gunner R MATTHEWS 109th Battery awarded the MM Captain JR COOPER joined for duty and took over the appointment of ADJUTANT to the 281st Brigade	
	12th		Captain JB GRAY joined for duty and was posted to command D281 CAPTAIN HAMILTON transferred to B281	
	15th		Major DYMOTT left for ENGLAND for a course of instruction School of GUNNERY. Captain HAMILTON returned from leave & is attached to command B.281.	
	23		Captain RT LEE returned from England & resumed command of A.281.	

WAR DIARY
or
INTELLIGENCE SUMMARY

Army Form C. 2118.

28¹ᵗ Brigade RFA

Place	Date	Hour	Summary of Events and Information	Remarks and references to Appendices
LAVENTIE	21ˢᵗ		Artillery School for 56ᵗʰ Division opened at LAVENTIE has commenced the day	
	23ʳᵈ		During the month there has been slight increased activity on the whole front. Hostile batteries at irregular intervals dealt with points E of the RIVIERE DES LAIES in the main communication trenches causing some retaliation on the Rouches + FAUQUISSART.	
	24ᵗʰ	7 pm	The batteries commenced with an interval bombardment by all batteries of the group on selected points. The bombardment continued with bursts of 5 mnr. until 8 am 27ᵗʰ December. There was no retaliation of any importance during the daylight. The enemy registered batteries with 77 mm & 4.2 mm	
	28ᵗʰ		Major H.G. FISHER proceeded on leave (21 days) CAPTAIN TARDIL assumed command of 109ᵗʰ Battery	

W.H.Geo.W.

ORIGINAL

CONFIDENTIAL.

WAR DIARY
OF
251st BRIGADE. R.F.A.

FROM 1/1/17 to 31/1/17.

WAR DIARY
INTELLIGENCE SUMMARY

281st Brigade R.F.A. Army Form 2118. ORIGINAL

JANUARY 1917

Place	Date	Hour	Summary of Events and Information	Remarks and references to Appendices
LAVENTIE	1st		Continued heavy shelling of GROUP FRONT during the day — apparently	
	3rd		Retaliation for our shelling of 24th – 27th ult. Lieut Col P.C.H. MACDOWELL R.F.A. assumed command of RIGHT GROUP being relieved of Lieut Col E.C. POTTINGER R.F.A. The RIGHT GROUP consists of 93rd, 109th, A/280 - A/282, D/282, C/282 Batteries R.F.A. The GROUP ZONE extended from DEVIL'S JUMP to SIGN POST LANE. LIEUT. COL. C.C. MACDOWELL R.F.A. comdg 281st Bde R.F.A. and H.G. FISHER, R.F.A. commanding 109th Battery R.F.A. were awarded D.S.O. and 2/87 Sgt. Maj. 34th Bde Battery and Bdr HOBDEN (who has since been killed in action) were awarded the MILITARY MEDAL in the field.	
	8		Heavy T.M. fire from German trenches on line of two heavy trench mortar positions. A salvo to retaliate was fired by our HEAVY ARTILLERY ... T.M.S.	

JANUARY 1917 WAR DIARY or INTELLIGENCE SUMMARY.

Army Form C. 2118.

281st BRIGADE R.F.A. ORIGINAL

Instructions regarding War Diaries and Intelligence Summaries are contained in F.S. Regs., Part II. and the Staff Manual respectively. Title pages will be prepared in manuscript.

(Erase heading not required.)

Place	Date	Hour	Summary of Events and Information	Remarks and references to Appendices
LAVENTIE	8		C/282nd BATTERY was heavily shelled today and fiven to lwanah the position. Talking up another in the Attynery area.	
			MOATED GRANGE, a very useful O.P. from which must of the ZONE could be observed was heavily shelled and rendered useless	
	14		On the nights of 14/15 and 16/17 C/282 BTY was relieved by C/260 BTY. MAJ. G.L. DYMOTT returned from Doncers Course today.	
	18		A raid was carried out by the 1/13 Battn LONDON Regt and ARTILLERY Support. Small raid with little success.	
	20		A raid was carried out an 7.0 p.m by the 1/12th Battn LONDON Regt. Artillery was asked to choose by many to take their if called upon. Anything was not requirdl.	
	23		The HOWITZER Batty (D/261) was made into a 6 gun Batty by the addition of 1 Section of A/282nd. HOW. BATTY. MAJ. G.L. DYMOTT assumed command of D/261 BATTY.	

JANUARY 1917

WAR DIARY
or
INTELLIGENCE SUMMARY.
(Erase heading not required.)

261st BRIGADE   Army Form C. 2118.

R.F.A.   ORIGINAL

Place	Date	Hour	Summary of Events and Information	Remarks and references to Appendices
LA COUTURE	23		Maj. S.W.L. ASCHWANDEN returned for duty from sick leave and was posted to command A/261st Batty.	
			Maj. H.G. FISHER DSO returned to the 3rd Army Class of Gunnery and assumed command of 109th Batty.	
			Lieut. Col. C.C. MACDOWELL DSO returned to ENGLAND in a GUNNERY COURSE	
			Maj. S.W.L. ASCHWANDEN assumes command of the 261st BRIGADE R.F.A. and Right Group.	
	24		A draft has arrived out of the 1/4th Battn LONDON REGT in Artillery and ordered to stand by but were not required.	
	26		The D.D.V.S. FIRST ARMY Army inspected all horses in the BRIGADE, his report was unanimously favourable	
	28		The 109th Batty was relieved by C/263rd Batty	

JANUARY 1917   261st BRIGADE
                                R.F.A. ORIGINAL

WAR DIARY
INTELLIGENCE SUMMARY
(Erase heading not required.)

Army Form C. 2118.

Place	Date	Hour	Summary of Events and Information	Remarks and references to Appendices
LAVENTIE	30		The GROUP Commander of the RIGHT and LEFT GROUPS changed commands this day.	
	31		Two batteries of LEFT GROUP were registered by enemy 4.2 hr. One section of B/262 BATTY left the GROUP. Considerable enemy T.M. and 5.9 activity took place during the night. Retaliation was requested by the Infantry and given.	

SgD Cookson Lt Col
Commanding 281st Bgde RFA
33rd Division.

SECRET.   ORIGINAL.

Vol 15

WAR DIARY.
OF
281ST BRIGADE R.F.A.
(LATE 1/2ND LONDON BRIGADE. R.F.A.)

FOR THE

PERIOD 1st – 28th FEBRUARY 1917.

Army Form C. 2118.

WAR DIARY or INTELLIGENCE SUMMARY

(Erase heading not required.)

281st Brigade RFA
1st / 2 London Brigade RFA TF

FEB. 1917.

Place	Date	Hour	Summary of Events and Information	Remarks and references to Appendices
LAVENTIE	2/2		B.282nd Battery relieved by A. 281 Battery. D 280. (1 section) left the LEFT GROUP.	
	3rd		Successful Aero registration in the snow.	
	3rd	7.45 pm	Offensive shoot on back areas. Heavies co-operating.	
	5th		Composite Howitzer battery formed (one section D281) moved to V Division area. 109th Battery attached to V Division.	
	6th		Offensive bombardment of back areas by night.	
	8th		German heavy bombardment on New Zealand Division (on our left).	
	10th		Left Group supported raid by 1st Bn London Regt on German trenches, no prisoners captured, but raid satisfactory. 109th Battery returned from V Division & their wagon lines and one section D281 rejoined at battery positions.	
	11		Inspection of Group front by CRA 56th & 5th Divisions and GSO 1st Div. XI Corps.	

2449 Wt. W14957/M90 750,000 1/16 J.B.C. & A. Forms/C.2118/12.

Army Form C. 2118.

WAR DIARY
or
INTELLIGENCE SUMMARY
(Erase heading not required.)

FEB 1917   281st Brigade RFA

Instructions regarding War Diaries and Intelligence Summaries are contained in F. S. Regs., Part II. and the Staff Manual respectively. Title Pages will be prepared in manuscript.

Place	Date	Hour	Summary of Events and Information	Remarks and references to Appendices
LAVENTIE	1st		Silent raid by 2nd Bn London Regt. no germans seen. Major FISHER joins for temporary duty XI Corps RA. 109th Battery and D 281 in action with Right Group 56th Div Arty.	
	3rd		No 44R. Sergt. T W HALL awarded the Croix de Guerre for gallantry in the SOMME Offensive Shoot on back areas HQ's, dumps & O/kerrine. General Carey GOC RA XI Corps visited OP's.	
	4th 5th 6th 7th		Left Group surprised raid of L.R.B. by barrage fire D 281 (one section) joined its group. Col C C MACDOWELL DSO returned from Overseas Artillery School and assumed command of Left Group. Major ASCHWANDEN assumes command of A 281. Major LEE assumes command of B 281.	
	18th		109th Battery relieves enfilade section A 281.	

Army Form C. 2118.

WAR DIARY or INTELLIGENCE SUMMARY

(Erase heading not required.)

FEB. 1917.   **281 Brigade RFA**

Place	Date	Hour	Summary of Events and Information	Remarks and references to Appendices
LAVENTIE	18th		A281 Battery heavily shelled with 4.2's & divisional Counter Mortar opposite WICK SALIENT at midnight. Very successful. Same 200 yards of German gallery received. D281 bombarded in co-operation. Warning order received to move into 3rd Army area on 4th, 5th, & 6th March. 56th Divarty to be relieved by 49th Div Arty. Guns to be taken over in pits. B281 Lone gun in action at DEAD END LANE (100 rounds). A281 Lone gun in action in BEDFORD ROAD. Exhumation of LEFT GROUP southwards to WINCHESTER STREET. Readjustment of battery zones. C.280 joins the group. 4 guns Le Épinette ferme and 2 guns at PONT LOGY.	
	20th			
	23rd			
	24th			
	25th			
	26th			
	27th			

LIEUT COLONEL,
COMMANDING 281 Brigade,
ROYAL FIELD ARTILLERY.

SECRET. ORIGINAL.

War-Diary

OF

281st Brigade R.F.A. T.F.

(LATE 1/2nd CITY OF LONDON BRIGADE R.F.A T.F.)

FOR THE PERIOD

1st to 31st MARCH.

1917.

Army Form C. 2118.

WAR DIARY or INTELLIGENCE SUMMARY

281st Brigade RFA
1st/2nd London Brigade, RFA TF

March 1917

Place	Date	Hour	Summary of Events and Information	Remarks and references to Appendices
LAVENTIE	3rd		O.C. and Battery commanders, 246 Brigade RFA, 49 Division reconnoitred battery positions and OP's with a view to taking over the line covered by 281st Brigade.	
	4th		Four Portuguese officers attached to the Brigade. On the night of the 4/5th, two sections per battery relieved by the 246 Brigade RFA and marched to CALONNE.	
	5th		Remaining sections marched to CALONNE on being relieved. Group command handed over to O.C. 246 Brigade, and Brigade HQ moved to CALONNE.	
CALONNE	6th– 7th		Brigade remained at CALONNE.	
			Brigade marched to LIETTRES (A.281 in ESTRÉE BLANCHE) via BUSNES and LILLERS, there billeted.	
LIETTRES	8th		Brigade marched to HEUCHIN via FEBVIN-PALFART, were billeted.	
HEUCHIN	9th		Brigade marched to CONCHY and MONCHEL picking up the guns of the 246 Brigade at BOUBERS.	

Army Form C. 2118.

WAR DIARY
or
INTELLIGENCE SUMMARY

281st Brigade RFA

(Erase heading not required.)

Place	Date	Hour	Summary of Events and Information	Remarks and references to Appendices
CONCHY	10th		Brigade marched to LUCHEUX via FREVENT and there billetted	
"	11th		OC and battery commanders reconnoitred positions on ARRAS battery over lines and	
"	12th		Brigade marched to SIMONCOURT taking over lines and billets of 145th Div Arty (46th Brigade at that place	
"	13th		Brigade Headquarters moved from SIMONCOURT to No 1 REE BEFFARA, ARRAS, one section per battery came into action on outskirts of ARRAS	
ARRAS	14th		Remaining sections came in action, forming 56th Divisional Artillery Group, covering the 167th Left Brigade. Zone from the salient N of BEAURAINS to the cross roads 1000 yards S of the village 14th Div Arty on Left, 35th Div Arty on right	
"	15th		Registration of all batteries. 4 building of battery positions. 109th Battery 4 men killed and 2 wounded in their position near the STATION ARRAS.	

Army Form C. 2118.

WAR DIARY
or
INTELLIGENCE SUMMARY

(Erase heading not required.)

281 Bde RFA

MARCH

Instructions regarding War Diaries and Intelligence Summaries are contained in F.S. Regs., Part II. and the Staff Manual respectively. Title Pages will be prepared in manuscript.

Place	Date	Hour	Summary of Events and Information	Remarks and references to Appendices
ARRAS	17th		A.281 battery 1 killed and 2 wounded at battery position (STONEMASON'S YARD near STATION)	
"	18		The enemy evacuated BEAURAINS. village occupied by our patrols. Infantry front line established E of BEAURAINS. enemy heavily shelled the village. Continued advance by our infantry towards NEUVILLE VITASSE. 281 Bde: KAY and HOLLIS accompanied infantry forward. Night of 18th. B.281 battery moved forward to position behind embankment E of ACHICOURT	
"	19th		All batteries active on NEUVILLE VITASSE and area. enemy shelling of ARRAS by enemy's heavy guns continued and gradual reconnaissance of advanced battery positions in enemy's heavy guns. O.C. made reconnaissance of advanced battery positions in our own front line and enemy's line under BEAURAINS	

WAR DIARY

INTELLIGENCE SUMMARY

281 Brigade RFA

Army Form C. 2118.

Place	Date	Hour	Summary of Events and Information	Remarks and references to Appendices
ARRAS.	19		One section of each battery (except B 281) came into action on BUCQUOY, near BEAURAINS. Infantry patrols report NEUVILLE VITASSE strongly occupied by enemy considerable work being done on its defences and wire. Group HQrs established in dugouts 500 yds W of BUCQUOY ROAD. 104th Battery (two remaining sections) advanced to forward position	
BEAURAINS.	22.		D/281 brought forward another section.	
	23.		A 281 moved two remaining sections forward. OC reconnoitred position for 293rd Brigade RFA under BEAURAINS	
	24.		B 281 moved forward to E of BUCQUOY ROAD under BEAURAINS	
	25.		B 281 shelled by 4.2's two guns hit, one out of action. Trail cut off.	
	25.		Work commenced on wire in front of NEUVILLE range extension but some damage done to wire.	
	25.		E/232 battery joined the MACART Group (281st Brigade RFA	

WAR DIARY or INTELLIGENCE SUMMARY

181 Brigade RFA

Army Form C. 2118.

MARCH

Place	Date	Hour	Summary of Events and Information	Remarks and references to Appendices
BEAURAINS	28		Night firing & wire cutting continued from day to day with indifferent results.	
"	29.		Reconnaissance made of forward positions for advance during operations, sites for positions of batteries selected.	
"	30.		Forward positions approved by G.O.C. R.A. 56th Division work commenced on them.	
"	31st		Dumps of ammunition erected at forward positions 300 rounds per gun, 1000 per gun at present position work on roads & battery positions continued	

Machun

SECRET   ORIGINAL.

WAR DIARY

OF

281st BRIGADE R.F.A. T.F.
LATE 1st/2nd LONDON BRIGADE R.F.A.T.F.

FOR THE PERIOD

APRIL 1st to 30th 1917.

WAR DIARY or INTELLIGENCE SUMMARY

Army Form C. 2118.

261st BRIGADE R.F.A.
(2nd London Brigade R.F.A.)

Place	Date	Hour	Summary of Events and Information	Remarks and references to Appendices
BEAURAINS	1.4.17 to 4.4.17		Wire cutting by all Batteries was continued on wire in front of W & N.W approaches of NEVILLE VITASSE. 4.5 Howitzer cooperated in the work. Wire lanes in all were cut by the Brigade. Expenditure of Ammunition was high owing to the length of range at which the operations were carried out.	Ref MAP 51.B.S.W. EDITION 4.A. 1:20000 FRANCE.
	5.4.17 to 8.4.17		Wire cutting operations continued. Barrage practised in cooperation with planes. By aero. Bombardments during the period was continuous on trench areas of NEVILLE VITASSE & communication trenches and lanes cut in more than shifted.	
	9.4.17		General Attack. ZERO being 5.30 a.m. Objective of 56th Div. was VANCOURT. The Brigade cooperated attack by 168th Infantry Brigade which advanced behind a creeping barrage. The enemy front line and the village of NEVILLE VITASSE was captured without difficulty, and few casualties. That the trench system in N.20 and N.21 further more difficult, the objective not being reached as the west of the day. After the capture of NEVILLE VITASSE the barrage was carried on by 250: Brigade R.F.A. 9th 261st Brigade R.F.A. moving into forward positions on M.23 – W of BEAURAINS – MERCATEL Road. This move was carried out expeditiously and without opposition. Hostile shelling with gas shells after the positions were reached. Gas defensive measures were taken and no casualties were caused.	
	10.4.17		Operations were continued. VANCOURT LINE and OOJEUL SWITCH SYSTEM were captured but enemy still held HILL 90 (S.W of VANCOURT)	

Army Form C. 2118.

WAR DIARY
or
INTELLIGENCE SUMMARY

281st BRIGADE R.F.A / 2nd LONDON BRIGADE R.F.A

(Erase heading not required.)

Instructions regarding War Diaries and Intelligence Summaries are contained in F. S. Regs., Part II. and the Staff Manual respectively. Title Pages will be prepared in manuscript.

Place	Date	Hour	Summary of Events and Information	Remarks and references to Appendices
HENDECOURT AGRACIES RLY ALLEY	[illegible]		Operations continued. Batteries advanced during the afternoon. No positions on N19c (S.W. of NEUVILLE VITASSE). WANCOURT village captured.	
NEUVILLE VITASSE	2.4.17		HENINEL and S.T MARTIN Sur COJEUL captured. Without further fighting enemy batteries withdrew during the night to S.T MARTIN. The advance was very rapid, owing to [illegible] Guns were found on NEUVILLE VITASSE – HENIN ROAD which had not been time to [illegible] and which no attempt to destroy. Heavy traffic [illegible]	
S.T MARTIN SUR COJEUL	3.4.17		Col. E.C.MacDonell assumed command of 58th DIVISION ADVANCED ARTILLERY consisting of 281st Brigade and 293rd A.F.A Brigade. H.Qtrs with Infantry Brigades in HENINEL	
	4.4.17		Orders by TE (approx 2.15 3.4.17 from 58 Division) to [illegible] SENSEE RIVER. Opening of offensive CHERISY ZERO 5.30a.m. Infantry advanced under enemy Barrage but positions were apparent. Attempt to [illegible] A.8 failed. A counter attack was [illegible] evening [illegible] our Sunken Road 0.25 a.c.d. but was caught by our own and enemy barrages and no [illegible] action of the enemy ensued by which our [illegible]	
	(4.4.17)		Enemy counter attacked about 8 p.m. regaining [illegible] to HARCOURT TOWER and [illegible] clearly by Artillery fire and put [illegible] Enemy Barrages failed.	
	[illegible]		58th DIVISION retained ground gained HARCOURT TOWER + SUNKEN [illegible] [illegible] to the [illegible] [illegible] retained [illegible]	

WAR DIARY or INTELLIGENCE SUMMARY

Army Form C. 2118.

251st BRIGADE RFA / 2nd LONDON BRIGADE RFA

March 1917

Place	Date	Hour	Summary of Events and Information	Remarks and references to Appendices
ST MARTIN SUR COJEUL	19.4.17		Considerable hostile Artillery activity on us from slightly from Light Gun - Heavy Artillery shelled St MARTIN SUR COJEUL throughout day. Our Artillery maintained a steady bombardment on all enemy communication trenches and roads	
	20.4.17		Harassing hostile Artillery activity especially on our roads and back areas. 2/Lieut HOLMASTER and 2/Lieut HG RAY and 3 other ranks wounded. 1 OR killed. Our bombardment of enemy communications continued	
	21.4.17		Few enemy activity.	
	22.4.17	4.15AM	Hostile raid on the RIGHT Battery opened on SOS lines, just did not reach our lines. MAJOR RT LEE wounded.	
	23.4.17		Attack by 3rd Army. ZERO 4.45 a.m. 251st Brigade RFA covered advance by 90th Infantry Brigade under a Creeping Barrage, on objective a line 1000 yds W of CHERISY. Attack did not succeed, from the heavy hostile AIF fire our troops could not carry the open. The enemy made a heavy plunge and had made a Heavy Barrage which commenced at 6.0 p.m. this open line and proceeded in reaching the sheep consolidation started at very heavy. 6 Bombs killed. 2/Lieut WH SMITH was killed whilst acting as FOO.	who blew up
	24.4.17		Enemy evacuated this position and retired on CHERISY. Enemy AIF war and 12.0 mm. was not opposed was greatly harassed by our own Artillery. At no the time was fight this operation from 12.0 mm to 20 R wounded. 2.0 R wounded	

WAR DIARY or INTELLIGENCE SUMMARY

Army Form C. 2118.

261st BRIGADE R.F.A.

2nd LONDON BRIGADE R.F.A.

(Erase heading not required.)

Place	Date	Hour	Summary of Events and Information	Remarks and references to Appendices
ST MARTIN	26.4.17		Enemy shelling the 18pr Batteries selected. Our howitzers & enemy commenced the R.F.A. roads at dawn.	
	27.4.17		A/261 Bty B/260 Bty and C/261 Bty attacked the 2nd Army Barrage on the 2nd June. C.O. noted of 2839 Rd 261st Brigade R.F.A. some wounded to the M/T & Dunne R.A.	
	28.4.17		A/261 R.A. Batteries of A/M9 and B/261 moved into advanced positions. Ammunition Supplied. Enemy Artillery Barrage instantly quiet. 60 R wounded.	

Sgt Auchraham
Commander R.A.
261st Brigade R.F.A.

SECRET. ORIGINAL 56th

Vol 18

WAR DIARY

of

281st BRIGADE R.F.A.

late 1/2nd LONDON BRIGADE R.F.A.T.F.

for the Period May 1st – May 31st

1917.

WAR DIARY or **INTELLIGENCE SUMMARY.**

MAY 1917

281st BRIGADE Army Form C. 2118. Royal Field Artillery late 2nd London Brigade RFA

Hour, Date, Place	Summary of Events and Information	Remarks and references to Appendices
1st May ST MARTIN-SUR-COJEUL (HINDENBURG LINE)	General bombardment of enemy's trenches and back areas. Wire cutting by 18 pr batteries on line NW of CHERISY.	
2nd May	Bombardment continued	
3rd May	General attack. Brigade covered 18th Division. Zero hour 3.45 am, advance was checked by enemy's machine gun fire and barrages. 2 battalions 18th Division however reached objective but were driven back by strong hostile counter attack from VIS-EN-ARTOIS. Enemy attack did not reach our line owing to our barrage. A second general attack took place at 7.15 pm again unsuccessful. Owing to enemy barrage at end of the day our position unchanged.	
4th May	Hostile shelling on back areas very considerable. 5.9 & 8" employed.	

MAY 1917   281st Brigade RFA   Army Form C. 2118.

WAR DIARY
or
INTELLIGENCE SUMMARY.
(Erase heading not required.)

Hour, Date, Place	Summary of Events and Information	Remarks and references to Appendices
ST MARTIN SUR COJEUL (Infantry Line) 5th May	Brigade active all day harassing enemy's movements. Very quiet in back areas considerable shelling on front & support trenches batteries engaged with success. Several active batteries with aeroplane observation. At 10.10 p.m. SOS reported, enemy barraged our front trenches at 10.45 pm all quiet.	
6th May	Quiet day. CRA 18th Division inspected battery positions	
7th May	Slightly increased activity on part of enemy waggon lines of brigade moved from AGNY to BOIRY-BECQUERELLE or COJEUL RIVER.	
8th May	Not any visibility, guns quiet, enemy guns shelled roads and back areas during night. Gunners JACOBS and LOFFHAGEN (B 281) given the Mil Medal for gallantry on the 23rd April	

WAR DIARY 281st Brigade RFA

MAY 1917

Army Form C. 2118

Instructions regarding War Diaries and Intelligence Summaries are contained in F.S. Regs., Part II. and the Staff Manual respectively. Title pages will be prepared in manuscript.

INTELLIGENCE SUMMARY

(Erase heading not required.)

Hour, Date, Place	Summary of Events and Information	Remarks and references to Appendices
ST MARTIN SUR COJEUL (Hindenburg line) 9th May	Enemy put down barrage on our front line. Probably hostile barrages as to our attack followed. Batteries dealt with back areas. Normal day.	
10th May	8" Hows (D281) damaged by splinters. Hostile shelling below normal.	
11th May 12 May	109th battery withdrew for one weeks rest. Divisional (18th Bdy) front increased. Enemy's activity at night shelling wrecks and battery positions gradually increasing, then number of guns has undoubtedly been increased during the last week. 8" Hows & 5.9" Hows deal with vicinity of Hindenburg line, while 4.2 guns deal with areas further back. All batteries and dumy useful work against small parties of enemy who venture into the open. Enemy becoming much less prone to show himself.	
13th May		

(73989) W4141—463. 400,000. 9/14. H.&J.Ltd. Forms/C. 2118/10.

MAY 1917

WAR DIARY or **INTELLIGENCE SUMMARY**

281st Brigade RFA

Army Form C. 2118.

Hour, Date, Place	Summary of Events and Information	Remarks and references to Appendices
S.MARTIN-SUR-COJEUL (Hindenburg Line)		
14th May	B 281 Battery forced to evacuate position owing to hostile shelling, no casualties. Battery returned into action in the am.	
15th May	Very quiet day. R.E. Signals joined the Brigade. I sergeant, 6 men.	
16th May	Very quiet day & night.	
17th May	Conditions normal, enemy still holds his front line strongly, & shews no sign of retiring his infantry or artillery. Col. C.C. MACDOWELL DSO resumed command of the Brigade.	
18th May	Increased enemy activity, back areas shelled with (lachrymatory shell) & 5.9's, roads & tracks HENINEL & HENIN dealt with by 4.2 gun	

MAY, 1917.   WAR DIARY   281 Brigade RFA   Army Form C. 2118.

or

INTELLIGENCE SUMMARY.

(Erase heading not required.)

Instructions regarding War Diaries and Intelligence Summaries are contained in F.S. Regs., Part II. and the Staff Manual respectively. Title pages will be prepared in manuscript.

Hour, Date, Place	Summary of Events and Information	Remarks and references to Appendices
St MARTIN-SUR-COJEUL (HINDENBURG LINE) 19th May	2nd Lt HOLLIS awarded the Military Cross for gallantry in action. Captain HAMILTON promoted acting Major & command B/281	
20th May	The 33rd Division made an attack on HINDENBURG Line S. of FONTAINE. Batteries cooperated. Objective was not gained. The enemy's artillery activity great on back areas during the attack. 6 men D/281 wounded. Night firing considerably increased. Following officers mentioned in despatches Major DYMOTT, Major HAMILTON, Captain WOLFE, Captain REID	
21st	Quiet day.	
22nd	D/Q battery moved from HENNINEL CEMETERY to a position on ridge above CHERISY near A/281 B/281	

WAR DIARY or INTELLIGENCE SUMMARY

Army Form C. 2118.

281st Brigade RFA

MAY 1917

Place	Date	Hour	Summary of Events and Information	Remarks and references to Appendices
ST MARTIN SUR COJEUL (HINDENBURG LINE)	23rd May		Little enemy activity	
	24th May		Enemy's battalion HQs shelled by all batteries good results - many casualties observed.	
	25th May		Enemy relief upset & dealt with by all batteries	
	26th May		MACART Group formed of A, B, C & D, 109th & 93rd batteries RFA to cover left-battalion front 18th Division during the day enemy activity unabatedly increased at 11.5 pm during of Summer alight by star shells & close to Brigade Headquarters 2 men killed at 2.30 Heavy shelling of our left-battalion by 5.9's all battery of Ammunition fired on SOS barrage. Shelling continued on both sides until dawn	
	27th May		Attack carried out on right of zone by 33rd Division. All batteries co-operated with smoke & shrapnel barrage	
	28th May		Quiet day, balloon registration carried out	

Army Form C. 2118.

WAR DIARY
or
INTELLIGENCE SUMMARY

291st Brigade
RFA

(Erase heading not required.)

Instructions regarding War Diaries and Intelligence
Summaries are contained in F.S. Regs., Part II.
and the Staff Manual respectively. Title Pages
will be prepared in manuscript.

Place	Date	Hour	Summary of Events and Information	Remarks and references to Appendices
ST MARTIN SUR COJEUL (HINDENBURG LINE)	29 May		Enemy's activity below normal. Kept attacks successfully attacked enemy posts in front of CHERISY and occupied them, enemy counter-attack dealt with and driven off	
	30 May		Quiet day, enemy's activity during night below normal	
	30 May		Group Headquarters moved 15 dugouts in sunken road 500 yards NW of ST MARTIN as previous HQs had been continuously shelled by 8" 5"9. 7th R W Kent Regt attacked & captured posts in front of CHERISY. Preparative bombardment by D 281 & 109 batteries. Results satisfactory, enemy had some 30 casualties from shell fire alone	

Signature
LIEUT COLONEL
COMMANDING 291 BRIGADE,
ROYAL FIELD ARTILLERY

To Headquarters,

      18th. Div. Artillery.

      I wish to bring to your notice the prompt assistance rendered by Capt. A. V. REID, 2/Lt. E. G. P. NATHAN and Lt. W. G. FOWLER and a party of men from D/281 Brigade, R.F.A in rescuing a party of men of D/82 who had been buried in a ruined dugout by hostile shell fire this morning.

      As the dugout - which had only one entrance which was entirely blocked - was small and crowded with men, they probably saved several lives, as the twelve men rescued were in danger of suffocation. Their work was carried out under considerable risk of further shell fire by the enemy and after a party of D/82 had been caught in that manner and suffered heavy casualties.

      I understand that Captain REID organised this relief party from his own battery which is some distance from D/82's position, and would recommend that his initiative and gallantry be deserving of immediate reward and I desire to thank him and officers and men of 281st. Brigade R.F.A. for their assistance.

      (Signed) A. THORP. Lt. Col. R.A.
28.5.17.   Commanding 82nd. Brigade. R.F.A.

231st BRIGADE.
R.F.A.

War Diary for Month of January

1919

Army Form C. 2118.

● WAR DIARY or INTELLIGENCE SUMMARY 281st Brigade RFA
(Erase heading not required.) 2nd London Brigade RFA

JUNE 1917

Place	Date	Hour	Summary of Events and Information	Remarks and references to Appendices
ST MARTIN SUR COJEUL HINDENBURG LINE	1st 2nd		Quiet day enemy did not interfere with our forward posts little artillery activity on either side, more enemy movement seen than usual	
	3rd		at 11.30 pm the enemy threw up rocket signals and immediately attacked our posts N of CHÉRISY preceding the attack they put down a heavy barrage just the right and then the entire post were attacked, the enemy captured the centre post a trench block prevented them proceeding up the trench	
	4th		at 11 pm our infantry (118th Division) attacked & retook centre post attack preceded by bombardment by 109th and D batteries and a hot barrage was put down by all batteries when posts were retaken. The enemy apparently substituted the newly occupied posts otherwise activity was normal excessive shrapnel and machine gunnery on posts during the night	

2449 Wt. W14957/M90 750,000 1/16 J.B.C. & A. Forms/C.2118/12.

Army Form C. 2118.

WAR DIARY or **INTELLIGENCE SUMMARY** 281st Bgade RFA

(Erase heading not required.)

Instructions regarding War Diaries and Intelligence Summaries are contained in F.S. Regs., Part II. and the Staff Manual respectively. Title Pages will be prepared in manuscript.

JUNE 1917

Place	Date	Hour	Summary of Events and Information	Remarks and references to Appendices
HENIN SUR COJEUL	5th		Continued shelling of our advanced posts & front line. 59, 42, and 47 fold guns used.	
	6th		HENINEL Valley heavily shelled during the early morning. CAPTAIN FARDELL 109th Battery and 2nd Lt NATHAN awarded the Military Cross in Sid Du(?) as Hd qrs degraded. Enemy still active against posts which are now consolidated. Headquarters Wagon line moved to Rest Camp HENDECOURT.	
	7th		A 281 relieved by C 280 and marched to Rest Camp. C 280 Enemy under orders of the MACART Group. HQ MACART Group relieved by 280 Brigade and marched to rest camp.	
	8th		B 281 and D 281 march in the evening to Rest Camp. C O and Adjt proceeded to HAMELINCOURT & report to CRA 21st Div A Cy (Brig Gn NEWCOMBE).	
	9th		CRA 56th Div A Cy inspected the Brigade in drill order. The inspection took place at 3.20 pm the General expressed himself pleased with the condition of the horses	

Army Form C. 2118.

JUNE 1917

WAR DIARY or INTELLIGENCE SUMMARY 281st Brigade RFA

(Erase heading not required.)

Place	Date	Hour	Summary of Events and Information	Remarks and references to Appendices
HENDECOURT	10		CO & Battery commanders reconnoitred new battery positions in the valley running NW from ST LEGER and HQ's in Railway cutting S of the valley. Brigade came under the command of the 21st Division from 6 am.	
"	12		Work commenced on new battery positions and Headquarters 109th Battery moved to new position	
"	13		new wagon lines reconnoitred 109th Battery wagon lines moved	
NEAR ST LEGER	14		HQ's & remaining batteries moved into action, a wagon line moved up to BOYELLES	
"	15		Registration of all batteries on area about FONTAINE and work on battery positions. Sunny day test barrages carried out in TUNNEL TRENCH	
"	16		at 3.10 am an attack was carried out on TUNNEL TRENCH FONTAINE by 21st & 58th Divisions, the attack was unsuccessful the company of the Right battalion only reaching the trench 2 creeping barrage	

Army Form C. 2118.

WAR DIARY
or
INTELLIGENCE SUMMARY

JUNE 1917 — **281 Brigade Royal Field Artillery**

(Erase heading not required.)

Instructions regarding War Diaries and Intelligence Summaries are contained in F. S. Regs., Part II. and the Staff Manual respectively. Title Pages will be prepared in manuscript.

Place	Date	Hour	Summary of Events and Information	Remarks and references to Appendices
SIEGER	17		Work continued on battery positions. Very little hostile activity. The brigade came under the 50th Div Artillery as from 1pm. Positions were reconnoitred by CO + battery commanders in the HENINEL VALLEY (HINDENBURG LINE) and batteries moved in during the night. A281 went in A46 in Sunken Road N of HENINEL, B went in C47 m/g HENINEL 109 in Hindenburg line S of HENINEL and D went to old position near COJEUL River between HENIN and HENINEL.	
	18		Hill batteries registered on CHERISY – FONTAINE area & later IQ w/m. MACART Group Headquarters established at a point in Sunken Road N of HENIN [at 46]. Bgde RFA HQ at 19 m/m. Considerable hostile artillery with 5.9s in HENINEL VALLEY in return salvoes, no damage done.	
HENIN SUR COJEUL HINDENBURG LINE				

Army Form C. 2118.

WAR DIARY
or
INTELLIGENCE SUMMARY

281 Brigade RFA

JUNE 1917

(Erase heading not required.)

Place	Date	Hour	Summary of Events and Information	Remarks and references to Appendices
HENIN SUR COJEUL and HENINEL	20		Registration continued and guns calibrated Lt N V BOWATER awarded the MILITARY CROSS	
	21		Wire cutting on the FONTAINE TRENCH commenced Gas bombardment by D281 on enemy points and roads about CHERISY.	
"	22		Wire cutting continued by 18 Pr batteries and gas bombardment repeated at night. Brigade zone increased owing to withdrawal of 114 Div arty from the line.	
"	23		Manoeuvre on night of June 30 by 21st Division attack on TUNNEL TRENCH HINDENBURG LINE unsuccessful	
"	24		Registration by B. and 109. Pr. Pendany attack on the FONTAINE TRENCH, CHERISY. A 281 Battery position heavily shelled by 5.9's & 4.2's throughout the day	

2449 Wt. W14957/M90 750,000 1/16 J.B.C. & A. Forms/C.2118/12.

Army Form C. 2118.

WAR DIARY
or
INTELLIGENCE SUMMARY

JUNE 1917   281st Brigade RFA

Instructions regarding War Diaries and Intelligence Summaries are contained in F. S. Regs., Part II. and the Staff Manual respectively. Title Pages will be prepared in manuscript.

(Erase heading not required.)

Place	Date	Hour	Summary of Events and Information	Remarks and references to Appendices
HENIN SUR COJEUL	25		at 9 pm. D & A batteries withdrawn to wagon lines. Brigade HQ Co withdraws to wagon lines in relief by 50th Div Artillery. B & 109 come under Tactical command of 251st Brigade RFA for operations commencing 11.45 pm attack on FONTAINE TRENCH attack successful	
	26		at dawn B 109 battalion withdrawn to wagon lines Whole brigade was assembled at wagon lines W of BOYELLES	
	27		Rest day	
HENDECOURT	28th 29th 30th		Brigade marches to rest camp at HENDECOURT. Inspection of horse lines by C.O. Inspection by CRA 56 Div of horse lines	

2449 Wt. W14957/M90 750,000 1/16 J.B.C. & A. Forms/C.2118/12.

SECRET   ORIGINAL

WAR DIARY

OF

281st BRIGADE R.F.A.
LATE 1/2nd LONDON BRIGADE R.F.A.

FOR THE PERIOD

OCTOBER 1st to 31st 1917

WAR DIARY or INTELLIGENCE SUMMARY

281st BRIGADE R.F.A. Army Form C. 2118.

1st (2nd London Bde) T.F.

October 1917

Place	Date	Hour	Summary of Events and Information	Remarks and references to Appendices
MORCHIES	1st		Corps Counterbatt'n Shoot on QUEANT area, all batteries took part.	
	3rd		Inspection of battery positions by G.O.C. R.A. Corps and C.R.A.	
	5th		Division of batteries into sections commenced with a view of repairing unit. Hostile battery activity.	
	6		A/281 moves one section to CAMBRAI ROAD near LOUVERVAL. B/281 moves one section to LAGNICOURT. A/280 goes out of action therefrom. 1 section attached A/281.	
	7		Gas projection carried out with field artillery fire, not satisfactory.	
	night 8/9		Small raid by London Scottish on MAGPIES NEST. S. of QUEANT to secure identification. Result unsatisfactory.	
	9		All batteries active on approaches QUEANT – PRONVILLE. Inspected roads.	
	10		Operations of 9th war repeated.	
	11		Gas shoot on MOEUVRES by D/281. 164° shelled 40 rounds 4.2 no damage to guns or personnel. Several rounds gas employed for registration.	

WAR DIARY
or
INTELLIGENCE SUMMARY.
(Erase heading not required.)

281st Brigade RFA.

Army Form C. 2118.

October 1917

Place	Date	Hour	Summary of Events and Information	Remarks and references to Appendices
MORCHIES	12/13		B.281. shelled Kringwat-the day. 300 rounds 5.9's found varying employed in conjunction with aeroplane observation damage nil	
	14		Lt Col S.W.L. ASCHWANDEN appointed to command 17th Brigade RFA 29th Division and proceeds to join Captain R.T. LEE to command A.281	
	15		Gas shoot on MOEUVRES repeated.	
	17		D 281 move from DOIGNIES position to position on CAMBRAI ROAD N of BEAUMETZ guns in either side of road from BEAUMETZ to MORCHIES in deeply sunken banks and invisible from above.	
	18		Inspection of battery positions by MGRA 3rd Army and QOCRA both expressed themselves highly satisfied with new battery positions	
	19		Reorganisation of Concentration + SOS lines.	

WAR DIARY
or
INTELLIGENCE SUMMARY.

(Erase heading not required.)

Army Form C. 2118.

28th Brigade RFA

October 1917

Place	Date	Hour	Summary of Events and Information	Remarks and references to Appendices
MORCHIES	20		Machine Gun Officers attached to batteries for the first time with a view to learning Artillery methods and cooperation of Machine Guns with Artillery in barrages &c	
	23rd		B281 Shelled all day, enemy's procedure as usual. Slow rate of fire & an increase with evidently longer with Sound ranging, increasing to G as MPI established on battery. Our batteries active. 250 rounds 59's and 42's dumped nr	
	25th		GOC RA Corps inspected battery position	
	28th		A281 shelled operation as usual. 500 rounds 42's dumped nr	
	30		Gas shoot on PRONVILLE	
			(several rounds in month —)	
			2/3rds of Ammunition expended by August. Light Railways brought up to use for ammunition supply to batteries. Tunnel dug-outs completed or all battery positions.	

[signature]

ORIGINAL

56 DH

War Diary

of

98th Brigade R.F.A.
(late 12th London Brigade R.F.A. T.F.)

From 1st November
To

NOVEMBER 1917

WAR DIARY
or
INTELLIGENCE SUMMARY.

281st Brigade RFA 1st/2nd London Brig RFA

Place	Date	Hour	Summary of Events and Information	Remarks and references to Appendices
MORCHIES	8th		10.0: Position severely shelled by sound ranging, no damage done. Some 150 4.2's and 5.9's	
	8th	12.40 am	Raid by "Rangers" on Magpies Nest S of Queant. Enemy artillery & trenches not affected, no prisoners taken, little hostile retaliation.	
	10th		Raid by 3rd Division on our left. No prisoners taken	
	13th		Wagon lines moved from HAPLINCOURT to FREMICOURT and BEUGNY	
	14th		Increasing activity of the part of the enemy. It does a good deal until battery positions, more movement observed on front and greater aerial activity	
	15th		The number of heavy & Siege batteries on our front is being gradually increased	
	16th		Attached section B 281 at LAGNICOURT whom to attry	
	20th		Attack by III, IV, VI Corps on HINDENBURG LINE S of MOEUVRES & BOURLON WOOD	

Army Form C. 2118.

(2)

WAR DIARY
or
INTELLIGENCE SUMMARY.
(Erase heading not required.)

Instructions regarding War Diaries and Intelligence Summaries are contained in F. S. Regs., Part II. and the Staff Manual respectively. Title pages will be prepared in manuscript.

Place	Date	Hour	Summary of Events and Information	Remarks and references to Appendices
MORCHES	20th		continued —	
			In conjunction with this attack, a feint attack made on Durvenal Front, between RIVER HIRONDELLE and LOUVERVAL dummy Tanks and infantry used. LEFT GROUP put down smoke barrage + wind fire on enemy front-line, with gas shell into village QUAENT and PRONVILLE Zero hour 6.20 am. Enemy retaliated heavily on Tanks & figures. All batteries active at night on approaches to	
"	21st		D281 and A281 move forward to LOUVERVAL Operations continued 109th Brigade reach HINDENBURG LINE Enemy reported to be retiring from MOEUVRES	
"	22nd		9th London Regt. pushes patrols out to keep in touch with 109th Brigade. Right batln 169th Brigade success in HINDENBURG LINE LEFT GROUP supports advance by smoke screen and barrage 169th Brigade attack enemy S. of MOEUVRES	

WAR DIARY
or
INTELLIGENCE SUMMARY.
(Erase heading not required.)

Army Form C. 2118.

Place	Date	Hour	Summary of Events and Information	Remarks and references to Appendices
MORCHIES	23rd		168th Inf Brigade sent to HINDENBURG LINE and continue the attack on TADPOLE COPSE. LEFT GROUP support the attack throughout the day assisted by 6" 8" & 18" Howitzer batteries.	
	24th		Enemy counterattacked in positions at TADPOLE COPSE and took certain small trenches in their front line system	
			7th Brigade RHA joined LEFT GROUP and came into action NE of LOUVERVAL near BOURSIES	
	25th		Attack on HINDENBURG LINE continued by 168th & 4th Brigade. LEFT GROUP supported the attack, 280th Brig RFA and Siege batteries co-operated. 168th Brigade reached and consolidated new position in TADPOLE COPSE	
		3.30 pm	Enemy counter-attacked but did not gain ground they were seen to suffer heavy casualties from our barrage fire	
	26th		Considerable movement reported behind enemy lines all batteries did effective work in Hostile Battery area	

WAR DIARY
INTELLIGENCE SUMMARY.
(Erase heading not required.)

Army Form C. 2118.

Place	Date	Hour	Summary of Events and Information	Remarks and references to Appendices
MORCHIES	27th		Enemy put down heavy barrages at 6 a.m., 8.50 a.m. and 6.30 p.m. and 9 p.m. Left Group retaliated searching up from SOS lines. No infantry attack by enemy followed.	
	28th		Enemy made half hearted attack on TADPOLE COPSE attack repulsed. Much aerial activity by enemy. OP of Left Group established at the COPSE. 3" enemy barrage in area during day.	
	29th		Enemy's artillery still very active particularly batteries in QUÉANT – PRONVILLE area and NW INCHY on trenches and TADPOLE COPSE shelled steadily through day. Considerable enemy movement round INCHY and N. of MOEVRES batteries active day & night with little intermission.	
	30.		Much enemy movement – guns observed heavy counterattack developed at 10.30 in the line TADPOLE COPSE, MOEVRES, BOURLON WOOD. 10.50 SOS sent up from TADPOLE, a determined attack developed on this front but was repelled by LONDON SCOTTISH and intense artillery fire by LEFT GROUP	

Army Form C. 2118.

WAR DIARY
or
INTELLIGENCE SUMMARY.

(Erase heading not required.)

(5)

Instructions regarding War Diaries and Intelligence
Summaries are contained in F. S. Regs. Part II.
and the Staff Manual respectively. Title pages
will be prepared in manuscript.

Place	Date	Hour	Summary of Events and Information	Remarks and references to Appendices
MORCHIES	30		continued —	
			Enemy suffered very heavy casualties during the attack, AntK	
			As we advanced across the open from INCHY K MOEVRES	
			and in its flanches N of TADPOLE COPSE which were	
			enfiladed by our fire.	
			A front illumination was made from the QUEANT—	
			PRONVILLE trenches.	
		11.44	Two German batteries limbered up moving into action E of	
			INCHY were engaged with decisive effect by DKG1 and AA81	
			Teams scattered a wagon blown up. 8" battery completed	
			destruction.	
			All LEFT Group batteries worked incessantly through the day	
			on fleeting opportunities & movements of which there were	
			an enormous amount.	
			Enemy advance checked along the whole line, but seems to	
			be in HINDENBURG LINE east.	

Army Form C. 2118.

WAR DIARY
or
INTELLIGENCE SUMMARY.
(Erase heading not required.)

Instructions regarding War Diaries and Intelligence
Summaries are contained in F. S. Regs., Part II.
and the Staff Manual respectively. Title pages
will be prepared in manuscript.

Place	Date	Hour	Summary of Events and Information	Remarks and references to Appendices
MORCHIES	30		continued — Attack continued the whole day and from observation it appeared the Division attacked on the MOEVRES front alone, but in our case were their objective attained at 5.30 pm Batteries ceased fire after having been perpetually in action since 7.30 am.	

ORIGINAL

CONFIDENTIAL

WAR DIARY

281st Brigade R.F.A.

(56th London Div. R.F.A.)

December 1917

WAR DIARY

28th BRIGADE R.F.A. T.F. LATE 1/2nd LONDON BRIGADE R.F.A T.F.

DECEMBER 1917.

Place	Date	Hour	Summary of Events and Information	Remarks and references to Appendices
MORCHIES	1st	3:30 AM	All batteries fire on SOS protective barrage at the request of 168th Brigade.	
			On TADPOLE COPSE	
		4 PM	Enemy barrage South of MOEUVRES followed by attack: caught by intense barrage and driven back.	
		4:30	A/281 engaged by hostile 4.2" battery (400 rounds) One gun hit.	
		PM	3 men killed and two wounded	
	2nd & 3rd		2 batteries 291 Brigade are attached to the 91st and 40th Div Artillery	
			Action - Alert when A/281 : A/281 goes into action again	
			9 C.M.P.H.Q.	
	3rd/4th		2/Lt CC MACDOWELL DSO and HQ relieved by Lt Col CLARKE DSO R.H.A. and HQ. 168 Infantry Brigade relieved by 9th Div. D/251 back north to LAGNICOURT HQ 281st Bde detailed R.H.Q. MORCHIES	
	5/7		Relief of all sections in battery by one section per battery 11th, 13th, 58th	
	6/7		Batteries on firing again into action in turn Nor EUIL and	
			E 01ST 109 Battery into indirect service (3rd Div) at VAUX	
VAULX	7th		2/Col CC MACDOWELL DSO takes command of centre group 3rd RA	

DECEMBER 1917

WAR DIARY 281st BRIGADE R.F.A.
INTELLIGENCE SUMMARY

Army Form C. 2118.

Instructions regarding War Diaries and Intelligence Summaries are contained in F. S. Regs., Part II. and the Staff Manual respectively. Title pages will be prepared in manuscript.

Place	Date	Hour	Summary of Events and Information	Remarks and references to Appendices
VAULX	1		Consisting of 40th Brigade R.F.A. and 281 A/281	
			Relief of Batteries by 112th & 158th R.F.A. completed	
			Guns & XII rounds sent to MORY. 3/B & C/281 came under orders	
	2		Left VAULX. 3rd D.A. (41st Div) (NEWLANDS)	
			Arrived & went into B. BEHAGNIES	
			GENRE GROUP 3rd D.A. B/C/ MACDONALD will supply ration parties	
			Infantry Strong Points known as 4 outpost Posts	
			known from Front to Rear - ROMAN, FACTORY, 3rd & 4th - here require	
			2 Infantry & 3 men O.R. respectively	
			AMMUNITION called for throughout the night by infantry	
			Rifle attacks but by the end of	
			situation & defences of outpost line	
	3,4		No action of particular importance	
			No active operations. 182nd Brigade relieved 4 section	
			H.B. Brigade R.F.A. 6 F.C. Ruy	
			Staff Hall left us for BEHAGNIES	

WAR DIARY
or
INTELLIGENCE SUMMARY.

Army Form C. 2118.

DECEMBER 1917   281st BRIGADE R.F.A.

Instructions regarding War Diaries and Intelligence Summaries are contained in F. S. Regs., Part II, and the Staff Manual respectively. Title pages will be prepared in manuscript.

(Erase heading not required.)

Place	Date	Hour	Summary of Events and Information	Remarks and references to Appendices
NOREUIL	14th/15		Relief of Batteries and HQ completed.	
BEHAGNIES	15		Brigade marched to MONTENESCOURT, and there billeted its night	
MONTENESCOURT	16		Brigade marched to BERLES - SAVY and billeted. B/281 battery in BERLES, B/281 in BERLETTE, 169th in CAPELLE FERMONT and A/281 in FREVIN-CAPELLE.	
BERLES	17		Lt-Col MACDOWELL departed this day for England, and Major G.L. DYMOTT D/281 assumed command during his absence	
	18		Orders to go into action to relieve 175th Bde R.F.A. 31st Div	
	19		C.O. and Battery Commanders reconnoitre wagon lines and battery positions. Wagon Lines B/281 and D/281 move forward to ANZIN.	
BAILLEUL	19/20		One section per battery relieves one section per battery 168-169-170th Bde RFA in and near BAILLEUL, arriving 168 Bde position copy	
	20		Relief of 170th Bde HQ and batteries completed at noon. B/281 and D/281 in BAILLEUL heavily engaged by hostile	
	23		5.9 and 4.2" batteries. 3 guns hit, no casualties	

WAR DIARY or INTELLIGENCE SUMMARY

DECEMBER 1917   228th Brigade R.F.A.   Army Form C. 2118.

Instructions regarding War Diaries and Intelligence Summaries are contained in F. S. Regs., Part II. and the Staff Manual respectively. Title pages will be prepared in manuscript.

Place	Date	Hour	Summary of Events and Information	Remarks and references to Appendices
BAILLEUL	25		"A" Battery near M.23.d.4.8. 3000 yards S.W. of BAILLEUL	
	26		"B" Battery near M.23.d.4.8. 3000 yards S.W. of BAILLEUL	
	27		Enemy shelled back areas and headquarters.	
	28		"B" Sub (Killed in action 18.7.17.) 2nd Lieut.	
	29		9th TRENCH MORTAR BATTERY. Cpl.T.R. Cooper. Lt. C.S. Poole	
	30		2nd Lieut. WILLIAMS Boards town with MILITARY MEDAL awarded S. Williams.	
	31		228 BRIGADE R.F.A. Adjutant T.R. Cooper Lieut. C.S. Poole	

(signed) E. Edwards
Major

To HQ 56. Div Artillery   WG/2

Hereto is attached War
Diary of 281st Bde R.F.A.
for January 1918.
Please acknowledge.

1.1.18.   John N Motherwell
                           for O.C 281 1/18

SECRET   ORIGINAL

WAR   DIARY 281st Bde RFA

JANUARY 1918

WAR DIARY or INTELLIGENCE SUMMARY

Army Form C. 2118

JANUARY 1918   281st Brigade RFA

Place	Date	Hour	Summary of Events and Information	Remarks and references to Appendices

VIMY RIDGE

LEFT GROUP 185 DIVISIONAL ARTILLERY BATTERY positions

Batty. included valleys between LONG WOOD and
BAILLEUL E. batty. in BAILLEUL 100 yds above road
W. of BAILLEUL. D batty. on road W BAILLEUL full
of shell craters E Pond de four yards 400 yds between
Nook 400 yds W of BAILLEUL
10ms 25' B. battn was shown around E. LA TARGETTE
21st century. Shelled by 5.9s — no damage or casualty
Batteries received intimation) Wounded GM Knee
Major E.B. Burnett Wound (from GM knee
Capt S. Halliwell wounded DSO and bar M3 L/Cp/T &M
invalid Billets moved to ZOUAVE VALLEY 3rd Lt GM
Healey & 2nd Lt Buck horton to take Wounded. L.G.H.
BRIGADE ANTITANK emplacements E. of BAILLEUL surveyed
& Capt. A 281 Bde would have position of emergency
Lt Col in old position

JANUARY 1918

281st Brigade RFA

Army Form C. 2118.

Instructions regarding War Diaries and Intelligence Summaries are contained in F. S. Regs., Part II, and the Staff Manual respectively. Title pages will be prepared in manuscript.

WAR DIARY
or
~~INTELLIGENCE SUMMARY.~~
(Erase heading not required.)

Place	Date	Hour	Summary of Events and Information	Remarks and references to Appendices
[illegible]	9th		Captain A V HEAL awarded the MC for bravery at battle of CAMBRAI	
	10th		Enemy bombarded back areas intermittently including [illegible] the BAPAUME–ARRAS road and battery positions. Two 18 PRS. B 281 moved forward as ANTITANK GUNS	
	[illegible]		C.R.A. 63rd Division visited battery positions. [illegible] with 100 shell.	
	13th		One section per battery relieved by one section 63rd Divisional Artillery. All sections 281st Brigade thus relieved [illegible]	
	14th		remaining sections relieved	
	15th		HQrs moved to LATARGETTE. Group Command passed to 315th Brigade RFA (Col Eden)	
	16th		[illegible] moved to LATARGETTE	
	[illegible]		Batteries marched to AUBIGNY Area. [illegible] EAST of CAUCORT. HQrs to GAUCHIN-LEGAL	
	[illegible]		HQrs moved to AUBIGNY (CABARET-ROUGE)	

D. D. & L., London, E.C. Wt. W5…/M1672 350,000 1/17 Sch. 52a Forms/C/2118/14

JANUARY 1918   291 Bde RFA

WAR DIARY
INTELLIGENCE SUMMARY
(Erase heading not required.)

Army Form C. 2118.

Place	Date	Hour	Summary of Events and Information	Remarks and references to Appendices
AUBIGNY			Inspection of all batteries by G.O.C. 55 Division. All batteries commented upon - improvement of standing and wave fires, and training.	
AUBIGNY			Regular training programme laid down including individual Trench section shelling, Forming &c.	

M. Adamson
Lt Col.
Commanding 291 Bde RFA

281/2 Brigade RFA

War Diary

March - February 1915

FEBRUARY 1918.

WAR DIARY 282/at Bde R.F.A.
or
INTELLIGENCE SUMMARY.

Army Form C. 2118.

(Erase heading not required.)

Place	Date	Hour	Summary of Events and Information	Remarks and references to Appendices
AUBIGNY	1.		C.O. inspected D battery	
	2.		Battery training continued.	
	3.		C.O. inspected B battery	
	4.		Training continued	
	5.		No 930047 Sgt E.W.BURROUGHS & No 940156 Sgt A.T. O'CONNOR were awarded the CROIX DE GUERRE.	
	6.		C.R.A. 52nd Divn inspected the horses of the brigade.	
	7.		Training continued.	
	8.		Brigade Field Day. Skeleton.	
	9.		Training continued.	
	10.		C.R.A 56th Divn inspected the brigade in drill order.	
	11.		Brigade Field Day. Skeleton.	
	12.		Officers from each battery reconnoitred battery positions occupied by 312 H Bde R.F.A. 62nd Divn.	
	13.		Battery training continued.	
	14.		Lt Col. C.E. MACDOWELL D.S.O. proceeded to H.Q 52nd D.A.	

WAR DIARY 281st Brigade R.F.A.
INTELLIGENCE SUMMARY

FEBRUARY 1918

Place	Date	Hour	Summary of Events and Information	Remarks
AUBIGNY	14		Lt. assumed the duties of C.R.A. 56th Div'n. Major D. G. L. Dupret D.S.O. assumed the command of the Brigade.	
	15		One section of each battery relieved one section of each (battalion) of the 312th Brigade R.F.A. in the line.	
VIMY RIDGE			Remaining sections moved to wagon lines.	
BAILLEUL	16		3rd Bde R.F.A., 622 Div Art. took up positions in front of LEFT GROUP 56th Division (situated as follows:- A Bty. 4,400 yds N.E. of BAILLEUL. B Bty. 8 guns occupied one section behind old Cway embankment between BAILLEUL & LONG WOOD. C Bty. 4,400 yds N.E. of BAILLEUL, and one section at railway cutting one mile nearer BAILLEUL, & one gun (anti tank) 1200 yds N.E. of BAILLEUL. 109th Battery 4 guns in position in BAILLEUL. One section in BAILLEUL — D Bty. BAILLEUL. One section in sector S.W. of BAILLEUL. One section 1500 yards S.W. of BAILLEUL.	

FEBRUARY, 1918.   WAR DIARY   28st Brigade
                  INTELLIGENCE SUMMARY.   R.F.A.

Army Form C. 2118.

Place	Date	Hour	Summary of Events and Information	Remarks and references to Appendices

VIMY RIDGE
BAILLEUL/6   Railway cutting, one section in BAILLEUL.
                 The 109th Battery at the BAILLEUL section of D Battery were
                 tactically under the command of the Right Group.
                 Gp b H.Qs in Sunken Road 700 yards W. of BAILLEUL.
                 The 168th Infantry Brigade in the line.
                 H.Q. & Battery wagon lines moved to wagon lines
                 on ARRAS – BAILLEUL Road, two miles from BAILLEUL

17   During the afternoon, A Battery's forward position
                 was heavily shelled by 5.9's, + one gun damaged.
                 A Battery's forward section moved to main position.

18   The ARRAS – BAILLEUL road was heavily shelled. Our
                 heavy batteries retaliated.

19   The enemy attempted without success to raid a post
                 of the Division on our left. Our batteries opened at
                 slow rate on S.O.S. lines until Infantry Brigade
                 reported all posts quiet.

WAR DIARY
or
INTELLIGENCE SUMMARY.

(Erase heading not required.)

Army Form C. 2118.

281st Brigade R.F.A.

FEBRUARY 1918

Place	Date	Hour	Summary of Events and Information	Remarks and references to Appendices
VIMY RIDGE				
BAILLEUL	20		Hostile artillery active on BAILLEUL	
			One gun of A Battery moved into position by the railway embankment between BAILLEUL and LONG WOOD as an anti-tank gun.	
	21		Nos 1, 2 & 3 Sections MIA dropped 210 rounds 4.2 on ARRAS	
			BAILLEUL Road	
			No. 101562 Ct. HOLLIDAY T.T. D Battery killed. Nos	
			167,76631 Gr. IVISON F. 101/4 Battery wounded in action.	
	22		Party of recruits joined from V Regiment.	
	23		Lt. Col. C. MACDOWELL D.S.O. assumed command of the	
			Brigade.	
	24		No. 167, 2/Lt BAKER R.E. D Battery wounded in action.	
			Considerable amount of individual movement on	
			Enemy's horse lines and back areas of arras 9 P.M.	
			Hostile A.A. guns very active.	
	25		Hostile batteries firing on ARRAS-BAILLEUL road	

FEBRUARY 1918.

WAR DIARY 281st Brigade R.F.A.

or

INTELLIGENCE SUMMARY.

Army Form C. 2118.

Place	Date	Hour	Summary of Events and Information	Remarks and references to Appendices
VIMY RIDGE				
BAILLEUL	25		was located by group H.Q. The use of a 9.2 battery was obtained from the C.B.S.O. The battery arranged by group H.Q. & the Hostile battery effectively silenced.	
	26.		Lt Col C.L. MACDOWELL D.S.O. proceeded to H.Q. 56th Divn to assume the duties of C.R.A. 56th Division. Major G.L. DYMOTT D.S.O. assumed the command of the Brigade.	
	27.		About 400 Rounds 5.9. & 4.2. were fired into BAILLEUL. One gun 109th Battery was damaged. The battery was located & our heavy artillery retaliated.	
	28.		One gun of A Battery was moved into position on ARRAS-BAILLEUL ROAD, 400 yards S.W. of BAILLEUL as a roving gun, for purpose of night firing.	

G.L. Dymott Major
Comdg 281 Bde R.F.A.

56th Div.

Headquarters,

281st BRIGADE, R.F.A.

M A R C H

1 9 1 8

ORIGINAL.   SECRET.

WAR DIARY

of

281st BRIGADE R.F.A.

late 1/2nd London Brigade R.F.A.

for the period

March 1st to March 31st

1918.

281 BRIGADE R.F. Army Form C. 2118.

WAR DIARY
or
INTELLIGENCE SUMMARY.   MARCH 1918 -
(Erase heading not required.)

Place	Date	Hour	Summary of Events and Information	Remarks and references to Appendices
BAILLEUL	March 1st 1918		Reinforcing Brigade Officers (48 Bde. A.F.A.) arrived on a reconnaissance.	All map References of Trench Map Sheet 51.B. N.W. 1/20,000
E. of ARRAS	2nd		Reinforcing Brigade Officers (155 Bde. A.F.A.) arrived on a reconnaissance.	
	3rd		B. battery moved its forward Section from B.22.a.10.25 to B.15.c.2.5. D. battery detached a Section to H.2.B.12. to come under 280 Brigade orders. Enemy artillery active all day in our area shooting.	
	4th		Enemy artillery again very active. Captain N. M. FERGUSSON R.A.M.C. took the appointment of medical officer.	
	5th			
	6th		C.R.A. made an inspection of battery positions.	
	7th			
	8th			
	9th		1/13 R London Battalion (KENSINGTONS) raided enemy trenches about OPPY covered by artillery fire of Two Brigades. Wire cutting had been done for two days previously by D battery. Raid successful. 4 prisoners and about 20 enemy dead left in the trenches.	
			Summers Time introduced at 11 pm.	
	10			
	11			
	12		D Battery moved its guns from B.26.B.86.07 to B.21.a.36.70 during night 11/12.	

WAR DIARY
or
INTELLIGENCE SUMMARY.
(Erase heading not required.)

Army Form C. 2118.

Place	Date	Hour	Summary of Events and Information	Remarks and references to Appendices
BAILLEUL	March 13		D/Battery moved one section from B.26.B.56.07 to B.21.a.51.70.	
	14		—	
	15		Military medal awarded to GUNNER W. GRANT 109th Battery.	
	16		Brigade on our right raided enemy trenches at night without success.	
	17		CAPTAIN J.R. COOPER returned from leave.	
	18			
	19		Lt. Col. E.C. MACDOWELL D.S.O goes on leave.	
	20		—	
	21		Quiet enemy offensive started after a bombardment. This sector was bombarded but no infantry action.	
	22		Enemy active again action.	
	23		—	
	24		Enemy 5.9 battery in the open was engaged by D and B batteries & afterwards dealt with by an 8" How. Battery.	
	25		—	
	26			
	27			
	28		—	

WAR DIARY or INTELLIGENCE SUMMARY.

(Erase heading not required.)

Instructions regarding War Diaries and Intelligence Summaries are contained in F. S. Regs. Part II. and the Staff Manual respectively. Title pages will be prepared in manuscript.

Place	Date	Hour	Summary of Events and Information	Remarks and references to Appendices
BAILLEUL	MARCH 28.	3.30 am	Very heavy hostile barrage opened. Gas & HE shell of all calibres on 56th Div. front	
		3.50	Sent Artillery barrage & S.O.S. lines put down by Groups	
		4.15.	Uhlan's sector B/281 put out of action by gas & direct hits & HE on guns	
		6.0	A/281 shelled with gas shells	
		6.30	109 Suffer casualties	
		7.5	S.O.S. from TOWN POST	
		7.30	Group S.O.S.	
		8.5	Same reported — EARL MARQUIS LINE	
		9 am	S.O.S. TOMMY POST. Enemy advance by Hop Garage	
			Enemy reported in TYNE ALLEY to B.23.a.9.3.	
		9.15	Enemy reported in CLARENCE & BRUM Alley. D/281 barrage	
		10.15	167 of LONDON SCOTTISH advance from RED LINE to support	
		10.30	Enemy make hostile attack down CLARENCE TRENCH. D/281 S.O.S.	
			& Clarence reported to D.	
			Linesmen over up to Box Wagon Lines	
		10.35	SD Enemy infantry reported about B.18.c. ent'd — D/281 guns in Front	

WAR DIARY or INTELLIGENCE SUMMARY.

(Erase heading not required.)

Instructions regarding War Diaries and Intelligence Summaries are contained in F.S. Regs. Part II. and the Staff Manual respectively. Title pages will be prepared in manuscript.

Place	Date	Hour	Summary of Events and Information	Remarks and references to Appendices
BAILLEUL	MARCH 28	10.45 a.m.	Liaison officer reports we have beaten back up OUSE ALLEY to SOUTH DYKE.	
		11.15	RED LINE Barrage to 200× opened in Protection.	
		11.45	Enemy attack reported to be breaking up under 18 pdr. Barrage & rifle fire. A/281 Section S. of OUSE ALLEY.	
			General situation reported good. Right Brigade told our line 5 posts 500× in front of it.	
		12 noon	122 nd & D/281 Batteries stop shooting N of OUSE ALLEY in accordance with our own advancing troops.	
		12.10	Red line barrage ordered to be held at all costs.	
		12.15	Enemy reported massing in the front line. Enemy batteries advancing up open engaged with good effect by Group & teams — no guns.	
		1-2 p.m.	Quiet - much target practice by Group & teams.	
		2.10	CAPTAIN WOLFE reported wounded.	

INTELLIGENCE SUMMARY.

Instructions regarding War Diaries and Intelligence Summaries are contained in F. S. Regs., Part II. and the Staff Manual respectively. Title pages will be prepared in manuscript.

(Erase heading not required.)

Place	Date	Hour	Summary of Events and Information	Remarks and references to Appendices
BAILLEUL	March 28.	2.30	Another Aviation enemy attack.	
			Aret gradually quieten down.	
		5 pm	10/28 took behind ridge.	
			109 in B/28 in on, on on to left.	
			28 Division has orders to move up and CANADIAN Divn.	
	29		Shape of Group became Sub-Group to 4 - C.F.A. Brigade.	
	31	6 p	Sub Group become Independent on lines directly under 1st Canadian Div. Arty.	

R.L. Wyatt
Major
Commanding 28. Brigade P.F.A.

56th Divisional Artillery.

(Late 1/2nd London Bde R.F.A.)

281st BRIGADE R. F. A.

APRIL 1918.

APRIL 1918   281st Bugade RFA   Army Form C. 2118.

WAR DIARY
or
INTELLIGENCE SUMMARY. 1st & 2nd London Brigade
(Erase heading not required.)

Instructions regarding War Diaries and Intelligence
Summaries are contained in F. S. Regs., Part II.
and the Staff Manual respectively. Title pages
will be prepared in manuscript.

Place	Date	Hour	Summary of Events and Information	Remarks and references to Appendices
ANZAC RIDGE BAILEUL	1st		Our heavy artillery active in early part of day. Hostile artillery moderate but enemy aircraft unusually active. Enemy movement otherwise normal.	
	2nd		Wing & Divisional artillery activities active with little hostile retaliation.	
	3rd			
	4th		HQ & firing section HQ.A 1.C.d.1	
			Group Headquarters moved to POULAINCOURT	
	5th		Heavy hostile bombardment during early hours of the morning returned quiet day.	
	7th		Brigade relieved warning to move at 9 a.m. Relieved by 101st Australian Brigade. Personnel & Officers withdrawn to Nissen huts, and from there & moved up to Scarpe (Canadian Artillery Brigade)	

APRIL 1918.   288th Brigade R.F.A.
                                                1st Bde London Bde R.F.A.

Army Form C. 2118.

WAR DIARY
or
INTELLIGENCE SUMMARY.

(Erase heading not required.)

Instructions regarding War Diaries and Intelligence Summaries are contained in F.S. Regs., Part II. and the Staff Manual respectively. Title pages will be prepared in manuscript.

Place	Date	Hour	Summary of Events and Information	Remarks and references to Appendices
ACHICOURT nr ARRAS	8		Headquarters of Group established in ACHICOURT. Batteries in action as follows: 109 near Station ARRAS, A & B on railway between ACHICOURT and ARRAS, D. South of main Station including ARRAS offices & accommodated in cellars, guns camouflaged. General situation quiet.	
	10		ACHICOURT and group H.Q's heavily shelled during day. 288 Bde Buford formed left Sub Group Right Mais Group 55 Div arty Enemy on battalion in the line.	
	11		ACHICOURT shelling continues. Personal casualties incurred.	
	12		Situation quiet. Infantry of ACHICOURT relieved at night. Group Headquarters evacuated by shellfire, no casualties. Group Headquarters established in RONVILLE CAVES.	
	13		Condition of front quiet.	
	14			

April 1918. 281st Brigade R.F.A. late 1/1st South Midland Bde R.F.A.

WAR DIARY or INTELLIGENCE SUMMARY

Army Form C. 2118.

Place	Date	Hour	Summary of Events and Information	Remarks and references to Appendices
SOUVILLE SAYS ARRAS	18		Situation unchanged. Enemy quiet on Divisional front	
	19		S.O.S. fired by 168 Inf Bde. Barrage successful. No machine guns & very little rifle fire.	
	20		Enemy fired a S.O.S. which on the A.O.S. was observed to be SOS signal. Every 10 minutes. No reply on artillery. Very quiet at DAINVILLE round 1.30 am. Our teams one	
	21st		Enemy actively registering area around Arras Station in afternoon. Lt. R. G. McDOWELL R.F.A. observer wounded by enemy shell. SOUVILLE heavily shelled by 5.9's and 8". Enemy aircraft active. Otherwise little activity	

APRIL, 1918.

WAR DIARY or **INTELLIGENCE SUMMARY**

281st Brigade R.F.A. late 2nd London Brigade R.F.A.

Army Form C. 2118.

Place	Date	Hour	Summary of Events and Information	Remarks and references to Appendices
RONVILLE CAVES ARRAS	24th		169th Infantry Brigade carried out raid on enemy trenches S. of BOIS des BOEUFS, raid unsuccessful, left up by machine gun fire, casualties 1 officer 10 OR men, 10 OR wounded. During the operation of this raid enemy opened heavy bombardt on left followed by a raid, they did not enter our trenches but W. prisoners in our hands.	
	25		W. prisoners being reduced to a minimum under orders from Rues-day, all being reduced to a minimum under orders from XIII Corps, the reduction of our night & day firing seems to produce a corresponding reduction in the enemies fire.	
	28th		Sent raid with bombardment carried out in support of Canadian raid in NEUVILLE VITASSE, raid entirely successful, a number of Prisoners and machine guns taken & considerable number of enemy killed.	
	29.		Group Headquarters moved to 5.10 Boulevard Carnot ARRAS. 280 & 281 Brigades now form Right Group 56th Divisional Artillery	

WAR DIARY
INTELLIGENCE SUMMARY

APRIL 1918. Army Form C. 2118.

281st Brigade R.F.A.
for the month of March 1918 (War Diary 281 Brigade R.F.A.)

(Erase heading not required.)

Place	Date	Hour	Summary of Events and Information	Remarks and references to Appendices
BEAUVOIS & CERISY ABBEY			Troops rested at intervals during the month and when not at DOULLENS STATION and approaches to the city during the air raids. I am forwarding names of Officers, N.C.O.s and men recommended for operations 28th March 1918. Lt Col A.G.W.FISKEN and Lt E.P.HUDSON 2nd in Comd (now Sub) CORPS and 5 Military Medals. Extract from Report by Brigadier General LOCH 168 Inf Brigade. Appendix A.	Appendix A

LIEUT-COLONEL R.A.
COMMANDING 281 BRIGADE R.F.A.

APPENDIX A.

Extract from Report on Operations in the vicinity of OPPY,
March 28th/29th.1918.
By
Brigadier General LOCH, Commanding 168th. Infantry Brigade.

The covering Field Artillery, Group, 281st. Brigade. R.F.A., maintained its reputation in all respects.

All Batteries sacrificed themselves nobly to support and cover the Infantry and my best thanks are due to these Gunners for the gallant manner in which they played their part.

281st BRIGADE.
R.F.A.

XXC 3D

281 Bde RFA

WAR DIARY

WAR DIARY
INTELLIGENCE SUMMARY.

MAY 1918 281st Brigade R.F.A. late 1/2 London Brigade

Army Form C. 2118.

Place	Date	Hour	Summary of Events and Information	Remarks and references to Appendices
ARRAS RONVILLE CAVES	1st		Hostile artillery active on Arras Station and RONVILLE area. Considerable aerial activity. Group batteries active on enemy's trench system during the night	
	2nd			
	3rd		RONVILLE area again heavily shelled.	
	4th		enemy's artillery activity continues above normal	
	5th		Continued intermittent shelling of Station area RONVILLE and ACHICOURT situation quiet, enemy's aircraft	
	6th		active	
	7th		Quiet day, activity down to normal	
	8th		15 minutes bombardment of ARRAS with gas	
	9th		Captain Heal assumes command of D battery vice Major	
	10th		G. Dyrenfurth attached Suwamai Arty 1965	
	11th		Habarollis moved to BOULEVARD CARNOT ARRAS	

Army Form C. 2118.

WAR DIARY
or
INTELLIGENCE SUMMARY.

(Erase heading not required)

Instructions regarding War Diaries and Intelligence
Summaries are contained in F. S. Regs. Part II.
and the Staff Manual respectively. Title pages
will be prepared in manuscript.

Place	Date	Hour	Summary of Events and Information	Remarks and references to Appendices
BOULEVARD CARNOT			Infantry Brigade relief, enemy shelled road and surroundings. Relief evidently observed by enemy aircraft.	
	16		Enemy's activity below normal	
	17		Enemy's activity increasing during the night, very heavy	
	18		bomb aeroplane raids enemy over ARRAS on bombing raids	
	19		based on line LILLE - DOUAI - VALENCIENNES over	
			Intermittent shelling of station, roads RONVILLE and	
			ACHICOURT battery positions still immune.	
			ARRAS bombed at 1.45 am and 4 am and 2.40	
	20		hostile in all enemy artillery also active	
			167 Infantry Brigade carried out successful raid on	
			enemy trenches at 2 am under cover of heavy	
			artillery barrage, & destructive fire, 18" 980 & 2118	

WAR DIARY
or
INTELLIGENCE SUMMARY.
(Erase heading not required.)

Army Form C. 2118.

Instructions regarding War Diaries and Intelligence Summaries are contained in F. S. Regs., Part II. and the Staff Manual respectively. Title pages will be prepared in manuscript.

Place	Date	Hour	Summary of Events and Information	Remarks and references to Appendices
ARRAS BOULEVARD CARNOT	21st		Brigades RFA co-operated on a number of the enemy killed. Harrassers & MG burst back.	
	24th 25th		Situation normal. Enemy 4.6 How. Batteries fired on Cups. Concentration against TM emplacements & ammunition dumps on enemy front-line system, no dumps blown up. Enemy artillery more than usually active on my C.A.	
	26		Non-defensive bombers day and night. Enemy shelling continues in spite of our sharp retaliation. Gas shelling of our rear tramway & at stations.	
	27		Enemy's fire continues intermittently. Enemy attack expected south of SOMME and at YPRES. Registration of our artillery commenced in preparation for raid.	

Army Form C. 2118.

WAR DIARY
or
INTELLIGENCE SUMMARY.
(Erase heading not required.)

Instructions regarding War Diaries and Intelligence Summaries are contained in F. S. Regs., Part II. and the Staff Manual respectively. Title pages will be prepared in manuscript.

Place	Date	Hour	Summary of Events and Information	Remarks and references to Appendices
ARRAS BOYARD CARNOT	6.8.18		Enemy's retreat has now turned. He appears to be constructing a control line for positions on our front. His patrols and demolishing squads on our side he had contained observation posts.	
		11 am	Our Front trenches and forward areas were subjected successfully to machine gun & trench mortar (very many) fire. They inflicted casualties (probably 6 wounded) to 9 horses. Later in the day, the (Division) telephone exchange was hit (two times) in the (at Group WPA 250 m. N. of Bogale Ridge). About 9pm the 5th Canadian Battery (6 hrs XIX went into action, and another battery of 5 south and XVII North (Smith Battery) Group & relieving, and moving & occurring without suitable had some 50 casualties for many shells of the battery commanded by the trenches being demolished by artillery fire.	

Army Form C. 2118.

WAR DIARY
or
INTELLIGENCE SUMMARY.
(Erase heading not required.)

Instructions regarding War Diaries and Intelligence Summaries are contained in F. S. Regs., Part II. and the Staff Manual respectively. Title pages will be prepared in manuscript.

Place	Date	Hour	Summary of Events and Information	Remarks and references to Appendices
ARRAS. BOULEVARD CARNOT	29th		Enemy activity below normal. Wire received by Night Group Wandering Artillery for our co-operation during raid. Copy attached.	APPENDIX "A"
	30th		161st Sub Brigade relieved by 164th Sub Brigade in right sector of Divisional Front. During the day ARRAS & ACHICOURT again bombed by enemy aeroplanes.	

31st May 1918
S. McLeod

W. Macdonald
LIEUT-COLONEL R.A.
COMMANDING 281 BRIGADE R.F.A.

Appendix A

G.S/48.

COPY.

C.C. RIGHT GROUP. R.A.

    Will you please inform all Batteries that supported us in the Raid last night, that all reports received from Raiding parties go to show that the barrage was first class, and must have inflicted heavy casualties on the enemy.

    Their trenches were evidently much more thickly held than usual, and the platoon and party leaders are emphatic in their statements of the number of dead Huns in the trenches, due to Artillery Fire.

    Their estimate of the number of killed and severely wounded Huns, due to artillery fire, was 200.

    The trenches were also very much knocked about.

    The protective barrage at the end of the raid was so effective, that the infantry came back in the bright moonlight over the open.

(signed). C. SMITH.
BRIGADIER GENERAL.
COMMANDING 107th. INFANTRY BRIGADE.

20.5.18.

SECRET   ORIGINAL

WAR DIARY
OF THE
281st BRIGADE R.F.A.
[late 1/2nd London Brigade R.F.A.T.F.]
FOR THE PERIOD
1st to 30th JUNE 1918.

June 1918

Army Form C. 2118.

WAR DIARY
or
INTELLIGENCE SUMMARY.
(Erase heading not required)

281st Brigade R.F.A.
(late 1/2nd London Brigade T.F.)

Instructions regarding War Diaries and Intelligence Summaries are contained in F.S. Regs., Part II. and the Staff Manual respectively. Title pages will be prepared in manuscript.

Place	Date	Hour	Summary of Events and Information	Remarks and references to Appendices
BOULEVARD CARNOT ARRAS	1st		Hostile artillery activity below normal. ARRAS Station and vicinity heavily shelled by hostile battery 5.9s at 5 p.m. and 9 p.m. 283 [Infantry] Brigade carried out successful raid N.Y. of [?] enemy put down heavy barrage upon [?] and support lines. No rounds before zero hour. [Casualties] [?] (1 captured) Hostile retaliation after raid.	
WAR AREA SIMONCOURT	2nd		Relatively successful [?] prisoners [?] No captured	
	3rd	4.10 a.m.	Enemy opened a heavy bombardment of our [front] line. S.O.S. at 4.15 a.m. down our own artillery barrage promptly. Raid by enemy attempted. Right Group co-operated with 11th [Bde] by Div Canadian Division long successful & prisoners taken. Hostile artillery activity below normal	

June 1918 281st Bde RFA (2)

WAR DIARY
INTELLIGENCE SUMMARY

Army Form C. 2118.

Place	Date	Hour	Summary of Events and Information	Remarks and references to Appendices
ARRAS.	4th		Group batteries dealt with enemys dumps (ammunition) in forward areas. One bomb dump blew up followed by twenty minutes. Enemy's activity slightly increased. Aircraft active. Major C. W. HAMILTON commdg B Battery awarded DSO. (Birthday Honours)	
	5th		Heavy artillery & 4.5 Howitzers dealt with dumps again. 4 blown up during the night. B.S.M. MARRIOT A 261. Awarded the DCM (Birthday Honours)	
	6th	9.40 pm	Enemy attempted raid on our right. (Canadians) raid unsuccessful left two prisoners in our hands 15th (Scottish) Division attempted a raid but failed to enter enemies Trenches.	

June 1918 A/81st Bde R.F.A.

WAR DIARY
or
INTELLIGENCE SUMMARY.
(Erase heading not required)

Army Form C. 2118.

Instructions regarding War Diaries and Intelligence
Summaries are contained in F. S. Regs., Part II.
and the Staff Manual respectively. Title pages
will be prepared in manuscript.

Place	Date	Hour	Summary of Events and Information	Remarks and references to Appendices
ARRAS	9th		Hostility was normal	
	10			
			Successful wire cutting	
			Gunner F J FEARN MM (wounded severely) awarded bar to military medal	
			Loyal N. Lancs raid on enemy's trenches carried out by 169th Infantry Brigade. Right Group co-operated. Raid strongly opposed. M.G.s from Buerke + Shrapnel house put down effectively. A.G.F. artillery barrage satisfactory, enemy had heavy casualties (40)	
			An Canadians carried out successful raid. Right Group co-operated. 1 officer 3 men & 1 m.g. taken, little or no hostile retaliation.	

June 1918   98th Brigade RFA

Army Form C. 2118.

WAR DIARY
or
INTELLIGENCE SUMMARY.
(H)
(Erase heading not required.)

Instructions regarding War Diaries and Intelligence
Summaries are contained in F. S. Regs., Part II.
and the Staff Manual respectively. Title pages
will be prepared in manuscript.

Place	Date	Hour	Summary of Events and Information	Remarks and references to Appendices
ARRAS	15th		G.O.C 15th Division inspected wagon lines and expressed himself pleased with all he saw.	
vergen huis SIMONCOURT	16th		Hostile artillery activity below normal.	
	17th		Hostile aircraft activity increased two enemy planes brought down one crashed in flames	
	18th		Quiet days in the line, little hostile shelling	
	19th		Enemy opened with hurricane bomb. advanced on important hostile lines, lasted five minutes, few casualties	
	20th 21st 22nd		Little hostile activity, two enemy planes over	
			BSM Willis 109th Battery BQMS Small and BQMS Oliver awarded the M.S.M.	

WAR DIARY or INTELLIGENCE SUMMARY

Army Form C. 2118.

28th Bn/Bugle
R.F.A.

Place: ARRAS

Date: 24th

Enemy's artillery & Machine Guns normal. Shell during 15th (Scottish) Bde (London) & 9th Canadian raided the enemy's trenches at various points and at different times during the night. Right flank raid got in all their raids but raids obtained their objects in a few places were taken & were under retaliation.

Raiders encountered 15th Scot Bde & 9th Canadian Bde in the trenches.

25th Enemy retaliation directed on front & support all known positions during day. Enemy's trench mortars (Minnies) active. Wire during day & no retaliation.

26th A warm day with a little increased shelling about locality of our & station by some hostile TM battery

June 1918

WAR DIARY
INTELLIGENCE SUMMARY.

Army Form C. 2118.

281st Brigade RFA

Place	Date	Hour	Summary of Events and Information	Remarks and references to Appendices
ARRAS	28		Inspection of wagonlines by OC, conditions entirely satisfactory, horses looking clean, well groomed & in good condition. All batteries good, condition of camps & huts good. A number of cases of an epidemic, like influenza, occurring in a GOC RA 56th Div Artillery tested 4 variations in Action in field (keen weapons). Results on the whole satisfactory	
	29		Front still very quiet.	

Macartney Lt Col Commander
281st Brigade RFA

SECRET

Original WAR DIARY

of the

281ST BRIGADE R.F.A.

Late 1/2nd LONDON BDE.

for the period.

from 1st July 1918 to 31st July 1918.

WAR DIARY
INTELLIGENCE SUMMARY

281st Brigade RFA lat 1/2nd London Brigade TF

JULY 1918

Place	Date	Hour	Summary of Events and Information
BOULEVARD CARNOT ARRAS	1st		Enemy repeated artillery hurricane shoot at 6.30 am on support line. Situation otherwise quiet, enemy's planes active
	2nd		Enemy's aerial activity continues
	3rd		Very quiet day - very little movement, no enemy registration
	4th		Harassing fire at night as usual
	5th		Slight increase in activity, both aerial & artillery
	6th		Raid by 16th London Regt. Group co-operated in dummy bombardment
	7th		
	8th		Very quiet day, little or no hostile activity, no enemy's balloons up
	9th		Back areas lightly shelled RONVILLE & DAINVILLE
	10th		Situation still very quiet, all activity below normal
	12th		During evening much individual movement seen, thought to be battalion relief, Group dealt with it's a centre of movement
	13th		Tranquility continues except planes more active

July 1918   281st Bde RFA

WAR DIARY
INTELLIGENCE SUMMARY
(2)

Place	Date	Hour	Summary of Events and Information	Remarks
ARRAS	13th		2nd Canadian Infantry Bugade relieved 169th Inf Brigade on left of Divisional front - situation quiet, relief successfully carried through	
	14th		4th Canadian Inf Bde relieved 167th Inf Bugade Command of front passed to 2nd Canadian Division	
	15		Slight increase in artillery during the night. Enemy offensive commenced from CHATEAU THIERRY REIMS to ARGONNE	
	16		Increase in hostile shelling & movement	
	17		Situation normal	
	18		Increase in hostile shelling ARRAS area at intervals during day and night. This increased shelling due to our increased movement (Canadians) & the activity of our heavy & siege batteries. 3rd Can Inf Bde relieved 4th Can Bde	
	19		Increased hostile activity during day, activity suspected in the enemy. All batteries active on CTs & Rds	

July 1918   282__ Brigade RFA   Army Form C. 2118.

WAR DIARY
INTELLIGENCE SUMMARY
(2)

Place	Date	Hour	Summary of Events and Information	Remarks and references to Appendices
ARRAS	19th		85th Army Field Arty Brigade (Canadians) moved into positions in group area covering the front SCARPE to NEUVILLE VITASSE to remain Silent Batteries.	
"	20th		Orders received to relief of both brigades of group by 277th & 311th Army Field Arty Brigades on the nights of 20th 21st (2 sections per battery) and night of 21st/22nd (1 section per battery) Teams of Army Brigades reconnoitre battery positions one section of batteries each wagon lines.	
	21st		Relief of all batteries completed by 6 gun guns taken over in situ. Personnel proceeded to SIMONCOURT Wagon lines.	
			Guns of 277 Brigade RFA. All batteries marched to ACQ and were then relieved by 282nd Brigade and two batteries 283rd Brigade H.Q.	
SIMONCOURT 22nd			in same area	
ACQ 23rd			Training commenced.	

February 1918

WAR DIARY
or
INTELLIGENCE SUMMARY

98th (Army) Bgd RFA

Place	Date	Hour	Summary of Events and Information	Remarks and references to Appendices
ACQ	24th		All batteries drill & [illegible] reconnaissance in SELO[?] area. Schools, gallery [illegible] as usual. 90th RA Officer inspected messes, billets and horse lines (himself very pleased with condition of gun lines.	
	25th		Drill continued in morning. began instruction in P[illegible] and Reconnaissance. Several Squadrons of 6pm in ACQ school. 90 & 56 Divs on Russian Front HQ. Two tons Mont de Poule ARRAS WE Hotel. Suddenly [illegible] for the gallantry with [illegible] [illegible] in ARRAS when two men of the Brigade were severely wounded.	
	26th		Gun & battery training continued	
	27th		Guns engaged at the PETEWAWA range	
	28th		XVII Corps Gunnery Exercise issued attendance [illegible]	

WAR DIARY 281st Brigade RFA
INTELLIGENCE SUMMARY

JULY 1918

Army Form C. 2118.

Place	Date	Hour	Summary of Events and Information	Remarks and references to Appendices
ACQ	29th 30		2nd Y Battery all batteries Orders received that the Brigade was to move into the line to old battery positions to relieve 1st Canadian Divisional Artillery (Left Brigade)	
ACQ	31		Section per battery moved to ARRAS waggon lines SIMENCOURT to commence relief.	

(Marshall)

SECRET   ORIGINAL

WAR DIARY

OF

281st BRIGADE R.F.A.

LATE 1/2nd LONDON BRIGADE R.F.A. T.F.

FOR THE PERIOD

AUGUST 1st to 31st
1918.

35807. W16879/M1879 500,000 3/17 R.T. (1074) Forms W3091/3   Army Form W.3091.

Cover for Documents.

Nature of Enclosures.

Notes, or Letters written.

AUGUST 1918. 281st Brigade R.F.A. 1st /d London Brigade

WAR DIARY
or
INTELLIGENCE SUMMARY.

(Erase heading not required).

Place	Date	Hour	Summary of Events and Information	Remarks and references to Appendices

MARŒUIL 1st — Situation normal. F.O.O. in ARRAS. Battery in position W. of Canadian Divisional Arty. Bivouac near Group HQrs. Brigade wagon lines remaining SIMONCOURT.

ARRAS 2nd — HQrs moved into old quarters in Boulevard Carnot & premises adjoining. Battery moved into action.

3rd — Situation at our front normal. HQ Centre Group moved to Brigade HQ towers left of Rue St Brigade. A.R.S. starting a picture of HQ's behind the front but movement in enemy's back areas considerable.

4, 5 — Enemy all quiet. A & B batteries but no instrument firing.

6, 7 — Enemy aeroplane over in vicinity of battery positions. Counter battery normal.

8 — Enemy aeroplane activity greatly reduced with our own. Information. A.A.A. Hostile Scouts attacked by our patrols. Enemy aircraft

August 1918 (2)

WAR DIARY
INTELLIGENCE SUMMARY

Place	Date	Hour	Summary of Events and Information	Remarks and references to Appendices
ARRAS	9th		Hostile aerial activity above normal. Otherwise unusually quiet.	
	10th		As for 9th inst. This condition of affairs continued for several days	
	14th		Enemy put down a barrage on the trenches of left Sector but no action followed. Hostile raid on protected	
			[illegible]	
	15th		Situation still quiet. Details of 78th American Division attached to 56th Division for instruction.	
			One platoon 71st Brigade 15th Scottish Division relieved batteries in the line.	
SIMONCOURT	16th		Battalion & company relieves arrived, & returned to SIMONCOURT	
	17th		Orders received to move to BERLENCOURT in due course. Musketry training commenced.	
	21st		Orders received for Brigade to move in action in BOISLEUX AU MOND	

AUGUST 1918.

WAR DIARY
or
INTELLIGENCE SUMMARY.
(Erase heading not required.)

Army Form C. 2118.

Instructions regarding War Diaries and Intelligence Summaries are contained in F. S. Regs., Part II. and the Staff Manual respectively. Title pages will be prepared in manuscript.

Place	Date	Hour	Summary of Events and Information	Remarks and references to Appendices
SIMENCOURT	22		Battalion recommenced 1500 to W of BOISEUX AU MOND Old buttons moved into Bdr. Headquarters established NNE of BLAIRVILLE 28th and 30th Bdes the former left group 56th Div, VI Corps	
BLAIRVILLE "B"			Attack by VI, XII, and Canadian Corps commenced. 56 Div found all objectives (QUEANT railway would forward to BOISLEUX ST MARC Group Headquarters moved to Quigula near BOISLEUX AU MOND.	
BOISLEUX AU MOND			Attack continued and work towards Junked by 56th Division. Posters moved forward to 98/EULES FONTAINE to BOIRY NOTRE DAME. BOIRY-S STATION. CROISELLES taken by 56 Division.	
	23		Enemy continued its advance towards rules of front North of CROISELLES (successful advance established at BOYELLES STATION.	

Army Form C. 2118.

WAR DIARY
or
INTELLIGENCE SUMMARY.
(Erase heading not required.)

Instructions regarding War Diaries and Intelligence Summaries are contained in F. S. Regs., Part II. and the Staff Manual respectively. Title pages will be prepared in manuscript.

Place	Date	Hour	Summary of Events and Information	Remarks and references to Appendices
BOYELLES	26		167th Inf. Bgde continued HQ attack	
	27th		167th attacked TOOLEY TRENCH all available guns. Batteries moved forward into valley between CROISELLES and ST LEGER. Guns moved to	
	29th		High Ground between CROISELLES and BOYELLES. Attack continued on BULLECOURT not entirely successful	
ST LEGER	30		Attack continued on ECOUST by 3rd Division made on STATION REDOUBT by 56th Durham	
	31st		Attack continued Right of 56th Durham consolidated in direction of QUEANT successfully dealt with by Right Group of 60 PRS.	

Muirhead
M.C.
Commanding 231st Brigade R.F.A.

War Diary

of
281st Brigade R.F.A.

Late 1/2nd London Brigade R.F.A. T.F.

for the period —
1st to 30th September
1918.

LIEUT-COLONEL
COMMANDING 281 BRIGADE R.F.A.

SEPTEMBER 1918

WAR DIARY
INTELLIGENCE SUMMARY.

281st Brigade RFA late 2 London RFA TF

Place	Date	Hour	Summary of Events and Information	Remarks and references to Appendices
ST LEGER	1st		The brigade put down E. of BULLECOURT to cover advance of the 57th Division, the brigade came under the orders of CRA 40th Division covering 52nd Division in the line and forming with the 280th Brigade, Right Group 52nd Div Artillery under command of Lt Col MACDOWELL the attack on BULLECOURT continued during the afternoon, and eastern edge of town cleared of enemy	
	2nd		Brigade continued the advance. 104th & B battery came into action at BULLECOURT. D battery at STATION REDOUBT. Lt Edwards D battery killed in action by a bomb.	
QUEANT	3rd		QUEANT and PRONVILLE taken by 52nd Division in the evening, Group Headquarters moved to QUEANT and Batteries into action between QUEANT and PRONVILLE 63rd Naval Division relieved 52nd Division in the Line Group coming under the 63rd Division as an Independent Group.	

WAR DIARY
INTELLIGENCE SUMMARY

(2) September 1918 — 281st Brigade RFA

Place	Date	Hour	Summary of Events and Information	Remarks and references to Appendices
QUEANT	4th		Hostility around INCHY-EN-ARTOIS and MOEUVRES enemy regained by a vigorous counter attack at 4pm a footing in MOEUVRES. Hostile shelling of QUEANT and area increased considerably. D & B batteries moved forward to within 1000 yards of PRONVILLE	
QUEANT	5th		Very quiet day, much less shelling our outpost line improved. Lt J C POWELL MC & Lt A C FISKEN MC wounded at OP. Brigade withdrew to ST LEGER out of action	
ST LEGER	6th		Brigade rested at ST LEGER. Heavy casualties. Three and 8 men caused by 5.9 HY shelling wagon lines. Brigade ordered to rejoin 56th division XXII Corps. Positions reconnoitred between ETERPIGNY and DURY	
ST MARTIN SUR COJEUL	8th		Brigade moved to ST MARTIN. Wire wagon lines were facing N over the SENSEE. established HQrs moved to BOIRY BECQUERELLE	

28th BRIGADE

WAR DIARY
INTELLIGENCE SUMMARY

(3) September

Place	Date	Hour	Summary of Events and Information
ETERPIGNY	9		Brigade moved in action near ETERPIGNY. Taking over from 25th Brigade RFA 1st Division. Headquarters in valley in rear of batteries.
"	10		Wire cutting commenced N of the SENSEE.
"	12		Hostile shelling on ETERPIGNY and CAMBRAI ROAD. General conditions becoming quieter.
"	13		Quiet – days little activity.
"	17		Brigade ordered to move to E of DURY and to take over from 3rd Canadian Divisional Artillery 9th & 10th Brigades. These positions reconnoitred.
"	18		Capt A V HEAL MC & Lieut AHZ wel wounded during reconnaissance.
DURY	19		Batteries moved into action about SAUDEMONT and RUMAUCOURT covering SAUCHY CAUCHY, C and du Nord. Headquarters SE of DURY.

WAR DIARY
INTELLIGENCE SUMMARY.

281st BRIGADE. R.F.A.

Date	Hour	Summary of Events and Information
DURY 21st		Forward positions reconnoitred for 109th A. along CAMBRAI ROAD 1000 yards nearer the CANAL
22nd		Quiet day. Area of village shelled. Major R.T. LEE awarded bar to Military Cross.
26th		A and 109 moved to new positions as instructed.
27th		General attack commenced by CANADIAN CORPS and XXII Corps. 11th & 56th Divisions front of attack between MOEUVRES and MARQUION. 11th Division on left moved after Canadian Corps Zero hour 5.20 a.m. 56th Division moved after 11th Division and after crossing canal du Nord astride the CAMBRAI ROAD and turned N. attacked along E. bank of CANAL XXI Corps captured SAUCHY CAUCHY SAUCHY L'ESTREE and OISY-LE-VERGER. 168th Brigade attacked N. along W. bank. Attack entirely successful. 56th Divisional line established S. of PALLEUL

285th Brigade R.F.A.

WAR DIARY
or
INTELLIGENCE SUMMARY.

(5) September

Place	Date	Hour	Summary of Events and Information	Remarks and references to Appendices
DURY	28"		Attack continued. Posts established N of PALLUEL and BOIS DE QUESNOY N of OISY LE VERGER	
	29"	12.30 am	orders received to prepare for attack on the line BUGNICOURT — CANTIN. Batteries ordered to move to S of PALLUEL. During the day all B batteries moved forward, and wagon lines moved from ST MARTIN-SUR-COJEUL to BUISSY (B. 109 D battery) and VILLERS LE CAGNICOURT (A battery) and batteries came into action in positions already reconnoitred. Preparations for operations subsequently cancelled. our patrols having had to retire from ARLEUX.	
	30"		Quiet day. Little hostile shelling with occasional of our heavy artillery	

C. Blackburn
LIEUT-COLONEL
COMMANDING 285 BRIGADE R.F.A.

Scout

War Diary

281st Brigade R.F.A.

(Late 2nd Kent (R.F.A. T.F.)

October 1918

WAR DIARY or INTELLIGENCE SUMMARY

98/2nd Brigade R.F.A. No. 19 London Brigade

Army Form C. 2118.

Place	Date	Hour	Summary of Events and Information	Remarks and references to Appendices
DURY	1st		Reconnaissances made of advanced positions between ECOURT ST QUENTIN and PALLUEL. ECOURT heavily shelled. Lt. E.P. HUDSON M.C. wounded	
	3rd		Batteries crossed the CANAL DU NORD by pontoons near SAUCHY CAUCHY and came into action SW of OISY LE VERGER. Right Group established in dug-out's near SAUCHY CAUCHY. 280th and 6th Brigades form the Group.	
OISY LE VERGER	4th		OISY LE VERGER shelled daily with mustard and High [Explosive] various calibres.	
	5th		ARLEUCHEUR attacked and taken by 168th Brigade but subsequently lost again	
	6th		ARLEUCHEUR again attacked and occupied. Immediately the night gun position established partly on E bank of CANAL DU SENSEE. In evening still holding ARLEUCHEUR	
	7th		Brigade co-operated in attack by 1st Canadian Division on the left	

WAR DIARY
or
INTELLIGENCE SUMMARY.

Sept 1918   93rd Brigade RFA   (2)

Place	Date	Hour	Summary of Events and Information	Remarks and references to Appendices
OSY-E-VERGER	3rd		1st Canadian Division Group forward ARLEUX & AUBIGNY-AU-BAC. The enemy artillery retaliated and was rather weak (some of had been for some time up to now) E.O.A. rather shelled with gas shell no casualties. The Right Group now composed of 8th AFA Brigade 250th and 93rd Brigades forming R.W. Brig. of (1st Can Div.) 5th Canadian Div. OSY LEVERGER entered. Enemy reported to be withdrawing along the whole line.	
	4th		Small scale patrols on F.N. bank of CANAL DU NORD. Enemy shelled roads & approaches to town OSY & FRESNES. Wind & weather fine during the day	
	5th			

Army Form C. 2118.

26/9/1918   98th Bde / or 98th Bde RFA (3)

WAR DIARY
or
INTELLIGENCE SUMMARY.
(Erase heading not required.)

Instructions regarding War Diaries and Intelligence Summaries are contained in F. S. Regs., Part II. and the Staff Manual respectively. Title pages will be prepared in manuscript.

Place	Date	Hour	Summary of Events and Information	Remarks and references to Appendices
OISY LE VERGER	11th		165th Bugade attacked and occupied FRESSIES 87 prisoners Left Group put down sleeping barrage in support Right Group now turned of 280°, 8° Canadian AFA Left Group of 26th and 155th Busad AFA ALBIGNY-AU-BAC occupied with little difficulty ALBIGNY-AU-BAC was taken by the enemy who retired to	
	12th			
	13th			
	14th		We regret on night of 13th 4 Canadian and 156th Bur all batteries of group active on ARLEUX and forced crossing near Hillage, group fire under 4 Cardin Bde on of CANTIN and BUGNICOURT	
	15th		Quiet day	
	16th		Headquarters moved to ECOURT ST QUENTIN Canadian Infantry (11th Busade) crossed canal at ARLEUX and PONT AU CANTIN enemy evacuated his area W of CANTIN and BUGNICOURT	

Army Form C. 2118.

WAR DIARY
or
INTELLIGENCE SUMMARY.

(Erase heading not required.)

Place	Date	Hour	Summary of Events and Information	Remarks and references to Appendices

October 1918 281½ Brigade R.F.A.

WAR DIARY or INTELLIGENCE SUMMARY

Army Form C. 2118.

Place	Date	Hour	Summary of Events and Information	Remarks and references to Appendices
MARCQ	20th		Brigade marched to ESWARS near CAMBRAI and was accommodated in the village which formed Army Reserve XXII Corps (in administration). Quiet on the entire front as far as could be heard. Refugees from DENAIN and VALENCIENNES passed through village.	
ESWARS	21st			
	22nd		Inspection of horses by CO. Quiet day. Section and battery training commenced.	
	23rd		Battery training in area round ESWARS.	
	24th		"	
	25th		"	
	26th		Ceremonial Training	
	27th		"	
	28th		Brigade marched to THUN L'EVÊQUE & THIANT and came under 49th Divl Artillery	

Army Form C. 2118.

WAR DIARY
or
INTELLIGENCE SUMMARY.
(Erase heading not required)

Instructions regarding War Diaries and Intelligence Summaries are contained in F. S. Regs., Part II. and the Staff Manual respectively. Title pages will be prepared in manuscript.

Place	Date	Hour	Summary of Events and Information	Remarks and references to Appendices
THIANT	29th		Arrived at THIANT and the Bugade was billetted in the area.	
	30th		Quiet day	
	31st		Batteries moved into action at MIANG enemy 49th Division as left Sub Group.	

(signature) Mackerel

WAR DIARY
281 BRIGADE
RFA
Month of November 1917

NOVEMBER 1918

WAR DIARY or INTELLIGENCE SUMMARY

281st Brigade RFA

Army Form C. 2118

Place	Date	Hour	Summary of Events and Information	Remarks and references to Appendices
MIANG	1st		Attack 5.15 am by 147th Inf Brigade, covered by 280 and 281st Brigade RFA closes, failed at 8 am.	
FAMARS	2nd		Batteries moved via MIANG into section of FAMARS S. of AULNOY, opened a barrage and then stopped as no opposition appeared.	
SAUTAIN	3rd		Brigade moved during the night to SAUTAIN. A battery in action supporting advance remainder in positions of readiness south of ESTREUX	
SAUTAIN	4th		The London Scottish attacked at 5.30 am supported by a barrage from 50 Div Arty and 147 Bgde RFA. A battery advanced with the infantry to M°Guire ground	
SEBOURG	5th 6th		A battery covered the line to Gnd HONNELLE remainder of Brigade remained in action on western bank. The 51st Divisional Artillery attacked the army and AVESNEAU Farms. Casualties Lt. M°Gregor gassed 345 + 346 Bgdes joined VG 56 Group RA	

Army Form C. 2118

NOVEMBER

WAR DIARY
or
INTELLIGENCE SUMMARY (2)

Instructions regarding War Diaries and Intelligence Summaries are contained in F.S. Regs., Part II and the Staff Manual respectively. Title Pages will be prepared in manuscript.

(Erase heading not required.)

Place	Date	Hour	Summary of Events and Information	Remarks and references to Appendices
ANGREAU	7:		167th Inf Brigade relieved 168th Inf Brigade during night 6/7: 167 attacked at 8.30 a.m. gained all objectives. Barrage put down by 245 Brigade and 246 Brig. RFA in action about ANGREAU. ANGREAU shelled with gas.	
HONNEZIES FAYT LE FRANC	8:		At 5 a.m. the Group moved with 167 Brigade to HONNEZIES. At 8.30 167: attacked covered by 245 & 246 Brigade. No barrage put down as no hostile opposition. HONNEZIES lightly shelled. Group moved same afternoon to CROQUET FAYT LE FRANC. 280 and 281 moved forward. MG area round HQs	
BLAREG NIES	9:		167th Inf Brigade continued its advance on QUEVY covered with Infantry. 281A & 280C moved forward HQs moved BLAREGNIES.	

NOVEMBER 1916 — 281st Bde AFA RFA

WAR DIARY / INTELLIGENCE SUMMARY

Army Form C. 2118

Place	Date	Hour	Summary of Events and Information	Remarks and references to Appendices
BAREGNIES	10		245 & 246 moved in support of 151st (B'gade) advance. Whole position W of QUÉVY. B'gade came into action CHATEAU WARELIES near QUÉVY, advance held up by each in wage E of MONS-MAUBEUGE 16 Lines altogether did not clear situation. Barrage put down by 145, 346 & 104th Battery. 63rd Division moved one B'gade North 151st Sub B'gade guarding night.	
CONVENT, QUEVY LE PETIT	11		Enemy's infantry retired on our advance. Some machine guns. Hostilities ceased at 11 a.m. 104 Battery in action on MONS-MAUBEUGE road 3 miles S of MONS from A/281 Battery (H.Q.) at 10.55 enemy retaliated on (A) battery position.	

Army Form C. 2118.

WAR DIARY
or
INTELLIGENCE SUMMARY.

(Erase heading not required.)

Instructions regarding War Diaries and Intelligence Summaries are contained in F.S. Regs., Part II. and the Staff Manual respectively. Title pages will be prepared in manuscript.

Place	Date	Hour	Summary of Events and Information	Remarks and references to Appendices
CONVENT QUEVY LE PETIT	12	—	The Brigade did not move forward, but batteries maintained their battle positions, moving their wagon lines up with the guns.	
	13	—		
	14	—		
	15	—	Official entry of 1st Army Commander into MONS. Five officers and seventy-two other ranks under command of Major G.M. Hamilton D.S.O attended this ceremony. Marching past the Army Commander after his entry into the City.	
	16	—	Officer	
	17	—	The Commanding Officer left for England on leave. Major G.M. Hamilton assumed Command of the Brigade.	

WAR DIARY
or
INTELLIGENCE SUMMARY.
(Erase heading not required)

Army Form C.2118.

Place	Date	Hour	Summary of Events and Information	Remarks and references to Appendices
CONLEM 19				
QUEVY				
LE				
PETIT	20		Bde moved from BLAREGNIES to FRAMERIES obtaining good quarters in a sugar factory	
	21		108 Battery moved from BOUGNIES to gently obtaining much better accommodation	
	22			
	23		9th Brigade about that day cleaning up and	
	24		carrying out repairs after the rapid advance	
	25			
	26		9th Brigade moved to HEVIEUX RENG area -	
			108 Battery in BERSILLES-ABET on outskirts	
			of VILLERS-SIRE-NICOLE in a large factory -	
			Bde DHQ in VIEUX-RENG.	

Army Form C. 2118.

WAR DIARY
or
INTELLIGENCE SUMMARY.
(Erase heading not required.)

Instructions regarding War Diaries and Intelligence Summaries are contained in F.S. Regs., Part II. and the Staff Manual respectively. Title pages will be prepared in manuscript.

Place	Date	Hour	Summary of Events and Information	Remarks and references to Appendices
MEAN-RENG.	27	—	Plenty of room for horses in the area occupied by the Brigade.	
	28	—	General conference. We held to arrange for men to obtain instruction in departs from ½ military to training.	
	29	—		
	30	—		

(signature)
Major
COMMANDING 281 BRIGADE R.F.A.

281st. Brigade, R.I.M.

War Diary - Month of December 1918

WAR DIARY
or
INTELLIGENCE SUMMARY.

(Erase heading not required.)

Army Form C. 2118.

281st Bde R.F.A.

Place	Date	Hour	Summary of Events and Information	Remarks and references to Appendices
CHATEAU ROUVROY	15th		Inspection of A/281st Battery by C.O.	
	16th		Inspection of 109th Battery by C.O. Telegram received authorising the demobilisation of any men on leave who & are in possession of certificate of employment from employer in whose service they were in prior to 4th August 1914.	
			During the month of December 26 men were officially demobilised and 49 other ranks joined the brigade as reinforcements.	

W Macdonald
LIEUT-COLONEL
COMMANDING 281 BRIGADE

DECEMBER 1918 WAR DIARY

281st Brigade RFA (London Brigade) TF

Army Form C. 2118

INTELLIGENCE SUMMARY

(Erase heading not required)

Instructions regarding War Diaries and Intelligence Summaries are contained in F.S. Regs., Part II. and the Staff Manual respectively. Title pages will be prepared in manuscript.

Place	Date	Hour	Summary of Events and Information	Remarks and references to Appendices
VIEUX RANG	8.5		All OC's marching the Brigade paraded for Inspection by General Outentin at VILLERS SUR NICOLE. 3 were selected for special mention, on being made.	
	9		Lieut Col. C.C. MACDOWELL returned from leave and assumed command of Brigade.	
CHATEAU ROUVROY	10.5		Brigade Head Quarters moved to the CHATEAU ROUVROY BELGIUM. Batteries remained as follows. 1094 Battery ROUVROY BELGIUM, A 281st Buttr Factory near VILLERS-SUR-NICOLE, B 281st and D 281st Batteries VIEUX RANG, FRANCE.	
	11		Inspection of B 281 by OC.	
	12		Inspection of D 281 by OC.	

JANUARY 1919

WAR DIARY
or
INTELLIGENCE SUMMARY

Army Form C. 2118.

281st Brigade RFA
1st/2nd London Brigade RFA TF

Place	Date	Hour	Summary of Events and Information	Remarks and references to Appendices
CHATEAU ROUVROY — BELGIUM	1st to 31st		The Brigade continued in billets in France & Belgium as follows:— Headquarters and 109th Battery. ROUVROY. B & D batteries VIEUX RANG. FRANCE. A battery GRAND RANG. BELGIUM. During the month a series of lectures on the British Colonies and other instructive subjects were given to the men of the Brigade, under the educational scheme, but beyond this little could be done in the way of education. During the month 2 officers and 64 other ranks and 109 horses were demobilized, including two parties of 50 horses each which were sent by road march to BOULOGNE for embarkation to ENGLAND.	

Machnell
LIEUT-COLONEL R.A.
COMMANDING 281 BRIGADE R.F.A.

February 1919   28th (or) Brigade R.F.A.

Army Form C.2118.

WAR DIARY
or
INTELLIGENCE SUMMARY.
(Erase heading not required)

Late 1/2 London Brigade R.F.A.

Place	Date	Hour	Summary of Events and Information	Remarks and references to Appendices
CHATEAU ROUVEROY 28th BELGIUM			The Brigade continued in billets in France & Belgium as follows: Headquarters and 1st battery ROUVEROY - BELGIUM. B/C batteries VIEUX-RENG FRANCE. A battery GRAND-RENG BELGIUM.	
			During the month 2 Officers and 50 other ranks and 100 Horses were demobilized.	
			A sale of horses was held at GIVRY at which 33 horses were sold from the Brigade.	
			6 men were selected for short service in the Army of Occupation.	

H. W. Gray, Captain R.F.A.
Adjutant, 281st Brigade R.F.A.

Commanding 281st Brigade R.F.A.

March 1919.

WAR DIARY
or
INTELLIGENCE SUMMARY.

281st Brigade R.F.A. 2nd London Brigade

Army Form C. 2118.

Place	Date	Hour	Summary of Events and Information	Remarks and references to Appendices
ROUVEROY.	11th		Orders received for Brigade to be reduced from cadre B to cadre A.	
ROUVEROY.	14th		Brigade moved to MESVIN. 109½ + HQts from ROUVEROY. A battery from GRAND RÉNG. B and D batteries from VIEUX RÉNG (FRANCE)	
	15th			
MESVIN.	17th		Guns and wagons of Brigade moved to JEMAPPES.	
	18			
"	29th		All ammunition of Brigade placed in charge. MONS	
"	28th		109½ battery (cadre A) entrained for ENGLAND.	
"	29th		Last horses of Brigade despatched to base.	

C Macdowell
LIEUT-COLONEL R.A.
COMMANDING 281 BRIG...

APRIL 1919.

WAR DIARY 281st Brigade RFA / London Brigade RFA TF

INTELLIGENCE SUMMARY

Place	Date	Hour	Summary of Events and Information	Remarks
MESVIN near MONS	6th		Three officers including MAJOR. G.L. DYMOTT. DSO and MAJOR. R W MARTELL and four officers proceeded to join Highland Division. 48 other ranks proceeded to 2nd Army RA Reinforcement Camp in Germany. During the month 20 other ranks were sent for Demobilization. The cadre of the Brigade remained billetted at MESVIN during the month.	
	30th		All battery imprest accounts closed and one CADRE imprest account opened.	

signature
LIEUT-COLONEL R.A.
COMMANDING 281 BRIGADE R.F.A.

WAR DIARY
or
INTELLIGENCE SUMMARY.

(Erase heading not required.)

281 Bde A.F.A. Army Form C.2118.

Place	Date	Hour	Summary of Events and Information	Remarks and references to Appendices
Quaregnon Belgium	25/6/19		H.Q., A & B. Batteries, 281st Bde R.F.A. proceeded to England	

A.C. Rowles
Capt.

NZP 27

CONFIDENTIAL

WAR DIARY

OF

....

FROM ....

TO .... 19.....

VOL. NO. ....

DUPLICATE

www.ingramcontent.com/pod-product-compliance
Lightning Source LLC
Chambersburg PA
CBHW081754220426
43649CB00038BA/3326